To Keri ~
for your years
friendship.

Carl F. Koel

PAPAS FRITAS TO FOIS GRAS

A MEMOIR

CARL F. KOCH

authorHOUSE®

AuthorHouse™
1663 Liberty Drive
Bloomington, IN 47403
www.authorhouse.com
Phone: 833-262-8899

Published by AuthorHouse 04/06/2021

ISBN: 978-1-6655-2170-3 (sc)
ISBN: 978-1-6655-2171-0 (e)

Library of Congress Control Number: 2021906821

Preface

PAPAS FRITAS **TO** *FOIS GRAS* **MEMORIES**

This book consists of 52 brief papers about events in my life between the ages of 6-65, some humorous some merely interesting. These were the years when my life was most fluid and eventful. Also included are several papers reflecting my personal philosophy (e.g. Touch the Water, Scars with Benefits).

Papas fritas refers to the dinners my mother gave my sister and me when no other food was available and are indicative of my early years. *Papas fritas* with fried eggs was one of my favorite dinners when I was growing up.

Fois Gras was included in a wonderful meal my wife and I had in Bordeaux, France when I was 65 years old.

All of these writings are much better because of my wife Joyce who patiently corrected spelling, grammar and asked questions about content. These rewrites resulted in a more polished final version.

Contents

The Prince George's County of My Youth

I WAS BORN in 1932 at Washington D.C.'s Old Sibley Hospital because it was the nearest hospital to the community in which my parents lived. We lived in Riverdale Heights, MD, a bedroom community of blue collar workers who were employed in D. C. The community was within walking distance of the end of bus service and this tied us to what we called "The District." Our community had only a small DGS grocery store and we did all other shopping along F Street, NW which we called "downtown." F Street had the 5 and dime stores, department stores, furniture stores and 7 movie theaters, 2 of which had floor shows.

We followed the Senators and the Redskins. We considered ourselves "Washingtonians."

We lived in Maryland and were also loyal to our state. Our schools and other social services were administered by the Prince George's County government. In 1928 the Baltimore Sun took note of the suburban towns growing up along the rail and streetcar lines in the direction of Baltimore but concluded that "Prince George's County is primarily an agricultural county" devoted to the cultivation of tobacco. I hope that the events of my life chronicled in this memoir show the evolution of P.G. County into a diverse economic county with 20th century values not controlled by rural "ruling class."

I attended Riverdale Elementary School and in 1938 we were in the first group to have dental exams and free milk. Elementary schools were seven grades and high school four grades. During the summer between my seventh grade and high school the state mandated that public education be 12 years. In 1950 I was a member of the first class in PG County to graduate with 12 years of public education. It was also the first class to play inter-high contact football and we won the county championship. The teams competing were: Maryland Park, Mount Rainier, Bladensburg, Hyattsville, Greenbelt and Laurel. All of these schools were either adjacent to D.C. or along the rail and trolly lines in the direction of Baltimore. At the time I did not consider what might be happening in the rest of the county.

Our congressman from 1939 to 1952 was Lansdale G. Sasscer, an Upper Marlboro lawyer, certified "don" and head of the Democratic Party. It was said that he was "the very embodiment of the seigniorial (feudal lord) system that ruled Maryland for generations". My father once wrote to Mr. Sasscer inquiring about the possibility of me being a congressional page. I do not recall the exact words of the reply but in essence it said "who are you and who do you think you are?" In the early 1950s Sasscer decided he wanted his son to be the state senator to the Maryland Legislature. The incumbent, H. Winship Wheatley was angered and started a reform group to challenge Sasscer, Sasscer lost his seat in congress and the reform group took over the Democratic Party. One notable member of the reformers was Gladys Spellman. In 1962 she became the first woman elected to the Prince George's County Commissioners and later became the chairperson. She became the congressperson from the 5th congressional district in 1975 and served until 1981. A portion of the Baltimore Washington Parkway is named for her.

But for the Spanish American War

T HE WAR BETWEEN the United States and Spain in 1898 led indirectly to my parents meeting each other years later in Riverdale, Maryland. At the start of 1898 neither were born yet and their parents were separated by an ocean. The probability that my parents would ever meet was about the same as the chance that you might win the PowerBall or the Mega Millions Lottery.

In the late 1800s my paternal grandfather, Frederich Julius Koch was a teenager living in Baltimore's German community. His father had emigrated from Wiesbaden, Germany and his mother Pauline Junger, born in London to German parents because her father was on a work contract there also emigrated from Germany.

My paternal grandmother, Ella Barbara Klein, was seven in 1890 and also living in the German community in the western part of Baltimore. Her parents had immigrated from the cities of Darnstatt and Neuremberg, Germany.

My maternal grandfather, Ramon Granados Marquez, who I always called *Abuelo* was born in Aracena, Spain where his family had lived for five centuries. His father was the governor of Huelva Province and owned a large property with olive and chestnut trees. The properties came to the Granados family in the 13th century from the king, Alphonso X, the Wise, as a reward for helping to free nearby Frontera de Jerez from the Moors. From that time on it was documented that the family was noted as a lineage of warriors with a few priests thrown in. Abuelo was neither. He was a university student in Seville.

My maternal grandmother, Concepcion Rey Capdeville, was a teenager in her home town of Seville. Her family can be traced back several hundred years to the late 1700s. Some of her ancestors lived in Seville and others moved there from Sanluca de Barrameda on the Mediterranean. This town is noted for having held the earliest recorded horse races and the races were held along the nearby beach.

The Paths to Washington, D.C.

Grandfather Koch joined the Army during the Spanish-American war and served with the 8th Calvary. He never left the U.S., but after the war he was sent to the Southwest to ensure that the Indian population stayed on their reservation. He never had anything good to say about the Indians in Southwest U.S.

After the war he worked for the railroad in Baltimore. He married Ella Klein and they later moved to Washington, D.C. because he had taken a job at the Naval Gun Factory in Southeast D.C. In 1908 my father, Charles H. Koch was born in D.C., the fourth of seven children. They lived in a row house at 1509 G St., S.E. Washington, D.C. The house was only a few blocks from the famous Congressional Cemetery where eighteen past congressmen, twelve senior Civil War officers and many other famous people are buried. Two of these other famous people were John Philip Sousa (died 1932) and more recently, J. Edgar Hoover (died 1972).

Beyond the cemetery to the east is the Anacostia River which at that time was a flowing clear water river before developments upstream began in the 1950s. These developments caused considerable sedimentation that silted up the river and caused its present tan coloration. It was along the river that my father learned to hunt, fish and trap fur bearing animals. In the process he also acquired respect for wildlife and a love of the outdoors.

Early in the 1900s and perhaps because he had served in the U.S. Army with men who considered themselves Americans without regards to their ancestry, my grandfather anglicized his name to Cook. My father is shown as Charles Cook through the fifth grade by the D.C. Public Schools but after that time as Charles Koch. It seems that his father was teased at the Naval Gun Factory for having changed the spelling of his name. At that time all things German were reviled, even sauerkraut which was called victory cabbage. In defiance of the prevailing public opinions, Grandfather Koch changed the spelling back to Koch but not the pronunciation.

When Spain lost the Spanish American War, one form of reparation extracted was that Spain would provide teachers to Cuba which had a very high illiteracy rate. My maternal grandfather, *Abuelo* to me, had a master's degree from Seville University and went to Cuba to teach. In 1903, my grandmother (*Abuela*) married her brother by proxy in Spain for the purpose of traveling to Cuba to marry my grandfather Ramon Granados Marquez. As a well bred Spanish lady she could not travel as an unmarried woman. My grandparents married in 1903 in Vinales, Pinar del Rio, Cuba by a priest. Their first child, Luis, was born in Cuba a year later.

The next three children were born in Seville, the last of which was my mother, Clara Granados.

Abuelo impressed the U.S. powers in Cuba with his abilities. One individual in particular was General Leonard Wood, the Military Governor of Cuba. General Wood encouraged Abuelo to go to Washington D.C. to teach government officials the Spanish Language. He opened the Spanish School of Washington in 1911. He also taught on occasion at the Georgetown School of Foreign Service and St. John's College in Annapolis.

He occasionally worked for Naval Intelligence during World War I. Several fact finding trips to South America to gather information for the Department of Navy were taken. During World War I he put put up maps of Europe at various D. C. hotels including the Willard and Old Shoreham. Each day he received information by cable from New York regarding the latest action on the war front. He would then go to each hotel and move pins on the map to show the latest advance of the armies. He was paid by the hotels for this service.

In July, 1911 *Abuela* arrived in New York with four children. Luis, age 7, Concepcion, age 5, Rosario, age 3 and my mother Clara, age 2. The family settled in a house at 14th and K Street, N.W. A fifth child, Ramon was born in D.C. but was of poor health. It was because of Ramon's poor health that they moved out of Washington. The family lived briefly in Mt. Ranier, MD where a sixth and seventh children were born, Maria and Delores. Another child was born there, Angelina who lived a mere 11 days.

On To Riverdale

The Granados family moved to Riverdale, Maryland in 1918. The house was a large Victorian house on the left bank of the eastern branch of the Anacostia River. The house was separated from the water by reeds and had a large backyard with a garden, chicken coop, rabbit hutch and a grape arbor. Three more children were born in Riverdale: Juan, Mercedes, called Beeno by family and friends and Antonio. *Abuelo* commuted to his Spanish language school by a streetcar named Mt. Pleasant which he boarded just four blocks away.

The Koch family moved to Riverdale in the early 1920s. The children attended nearby Riverdale Elementary School as did some of the Granados children. Later my siblings and I attended this same school which had been enlarged. My mother remembers that her teacher died during the influenza epidemic of World War I.

Grandfather Koch initially set up a blacksmith shop primarily to shoe horses. It is problematic how he learned this trade, perhaps he shod horses when he was with the 8th Calvary and he may have shod horses at the Naval Gun Factory since they undoubtedly used large horses like the Percherons or

Clydesdales to move the large naval cannon from one work area to another. In any event, increased use of the automobile caused the demise of his blacksmith business. By the early 1930s he had begun selling life insurance policies for Metropolitan Life Insurance Company. During the depression these policies were often small (one or two hundred dollars)—just enough life insurance to put you in the ground.

Neither of my parents went to school beyond the seventh grade. My father became a union printer and spent his early years operating a Linotype machine. He taught himself to play the guitar and banjo. On weekends during the summer months he played banjo in a dance band in Chesapeake Beach. In those days there was a railroad from D.C. to the beach.

My mother worked as a clerk for a tobacco dealer with a small office in the Grand Union Market off of New York Avenue which is now known as the Union Market. She sometimes went to dances at Chesapeake Beach with her friend Virginia Clair. She and my father became friends and she began riding to work with him daily in his car. Later they married and started a family in a small house on Charlotte Avenue in Riverdale Heights.

Two very interesting and very different paths were taken by the families to end up in Riverdale. That would not have happened but for the Spanish American War.

The Sword Over
The Archway

THE MOST VIVID image from my early childhood is that of a large battle sword hanging over an archway. The sword was unusual because the guard was not curved and was at a 45 degree angle from the grip. You can imagine such a sword was used by El Cid when he drove the Moors from Spain in the 1400s. The sword hung over the archway leading to the kitchen of the farmhouse. Other images allow me to describe the building and grounds.

It was a three storied wooden farmhouse in Riverdale on the northeast branch of the Anacostia River. The first floor was an above ground basement, the second contained the living, dining and kitchen areas and upstairs were bedrooms. The farmhouse belonged to my grandfather who immigrated from Spain in 1910. He was a language professor in D. C. who needed a large house because he had ten children and because his youngest child was sickly. A farmhouse in the suburbs with clean air was perfect.

From the front you saw steps to the second level and a large porch across the front and along the right side. The entrance door was left of center and entering there was a hallway with steps to the upstairs on the left, an archway to the kitchen straight ahead and another archway to the living room on the right.

The house sat back from the road and in the back was a garden, grape vines, and a chicken coop. The back yard sloped towards the river but a dense growth of reeds prevented a view of the river. There was a path into the reeds and I believe that trash was put there out of sight of the house.

At the time I was just short of my fifth birthday. My older by two years sister Clara and I were sent to stay at the farmhouse under the care of my Aunt Mercedes (called Beeno by all), age 17, and my uncle Antonio, age 15 because my mother went to the hospital to give birth to my sister Barbara.

My childhood memories are just images, the front porch, the hallway, back yard and the sword. The history of events I have learned during my life but the memories are actually a set of images similar to pictures of events in a photo album.

I have since learned that my grandfather had a stroke during our stay and died in his office. Clara and I returned to our own house under the care of Aunt Beeno. For reasons having to do with the strict Catholic church and the fact that my father was not Catholic, my uncle being the oldest of the ten children took over the house and I never saw the sword again.

About the sword, I guess it was a family heirloom that my grandfather brought with him from Spain. He was born in 1880, in Aracena, Huelva Spain to a wealthy landowner who was also Gobernador of the Provence of Huelva. The large parcel of land just north of Seville was given to an ancestor for service in wartime to the King. Maybe the sword was used at that earlier time.

Noting that my earliest childhood memory occurred when I was nearly five years old, must mean that my early childhood was peaceful and absent of notable events. Several people have described events that occurred at the age of three, but these events are remembered because a trauma such as being lost or being injured. I am grateful that my early life lacked drama.

My Name is Carl
K-O-C-H, Cook

WHEN I CHECK in at hotels or airport counters the first thing that the person behind the counter asks me is – what is your name, please? My stock answer is: my name is Carl K-O-C-H pronounced Cook and there is seldom a problem. I have learned the hard way that if I reply Carl Cook spelled K-O-C-H they immediately start searching under the Cs and never hear the spelling. It is a consistent pattern that I attribute to some quirk of human nature. In other situations it is asked why don't I pronounce my name as Coke like the well known billionaire Koch brothers or Kotch like the former mayor of New York. These problems have plagued me for eight decades and the story of why my family pronounces K-O-C-H like Cook goes back to my grandfather.

My grandfather, Fred Julius Koch was born into a German community in Baltimore, Maryland. In this community everyone was from Germany and German was spoken in the homes. The name Koch which means cook in German was accepted. After a stint in the US Army Calvary during the Spanish-American War he took a job at the Naval Gun Factory, now the Navy Yard in SE Washington DC, as a blacksmith. He lived with his wife and their children in a row house on G Street SE near Barney Circle, so called because the street car out Pennsylvania Avenue turned around there. This community was quite diverse and included people with Italian, French, Irish or West Virginia heritage. About 1910, he decided that his family had been in this new country so long that Koch should be anglicized to Cook and pronounced accordingly.

As a boy, my father grew up in that house on G Street SE. The area was called Congress Heights He lived just a few blocks from Congressional Cemetery where many famous people are buried. Among these famous people are 16 senators, 68 members of the house, two vice presidents, Matthew Brady, John Philip Sousa and J. Edgar Hoover. Just beyond the cemetery, to the east is the Anacostia River. The river was much different then than it is today. If I understand the things that my father told me, the water was clear and possibly non-tidal. The river basin filled later with sediment beginning in the 1950s when housing developments exploded in Hyattsville, College Park and other areas on the Anacostia River watershed. He learned to trap fur bearing animals and to catch the fish that ran up the river in the springtime. This resulted in his lifelong love of nature, a love that he passed on to me. What a joyous childhood he had in the shadow of the Capital Dome.

My father entered the DC public school as Charles Cook. When World War I came along, all things German were reviled. For example, sauerkraut was renamed victory cabbage. At the Naval Gun Factory, my grandfather's co-workers teased him about changing his name. Was he ashamed to be German?? That was too much for him to bear. In the middle of World War I he changed the spelling back to K-O-C-H but not the pronunciation. Public school records for my father list him as Charles Cook until the 5th grade and Charles Koch after that. A number of other people with the surname Koch pronounce it like Cook. I don't know why they do that, I only know the reason why I go through life replying– my name is Carl K-O-C-H Cook!

A Folk Song for Young Children

GRANDFATHER KOCH IS the only grandparent I fondly remember. My Spanish grandparents were both dead before my fifth birthday and Grandmother Koch did not demonstrate her affections, no hugging nor little *bises*. The two of them were born and raised in the German community of Baltimore.

My relationship with them seemed cursed from the beginning. One time I received my Grandfather Koch's butterfly collection that was framed and under glass. Before I got it home I inadvertently sat on it and it was ruined. Christmas gifts never resulted in something that I could enjoy. A toy violin that didn't make noise because it didn't include resin and a chemistry set that had a wooden microscope because of the war were a few of the attempts at showing love but neither could be used.

Although he died when I was eleven, one memory of Grandfather Koch that has endured is a folk song he sang to small children that he placed on his knee. He would bounce the child on his knee as he sang this song:

> Oh I sat miss mousie on my knee
> and a rinka pony ki no
> And I said miss mousie will you marry me
> and a rinka pony ki no
> Rinka pony stick stack stoney
> hump belly welly, hump belly weeeeeee
> At this point he would lift the child off of his
> knee
> And a rinka pony ki no
> Ducks in the attic shooting dice
> Spider in a web catching flies
> Nellie in the garden picking peas
> Come and kiss me will you pleeeeeeeese
> At this point he would plant a kiss
> And hopalong Peter and a hopalong
> Hopalong Peter and Wally sing a song
> Hopalong Peter and away we goooooooo
> At this point he would thrust the child high into
> the air
> And never come back on a gooseberry vine

I remember this song because I played it in my mind throughout my life. There are undoubtedly errors but who's perfect. I have no idea of the song's origin but it is most likely that he learned it as a child in the German community of Baltimore. It certainly qualifies as a true folk song under any definition.

"Relative" Regrets

I RECENTLY RETURNED from Bensalem, PA, a small town about 15 miles east of downtown Philadelphia where my wife and I attended the viewing of Antonio (Tony) Granados, 94. We did not attend the Mass or the burial. Tony was the youngest and last surviving child of the ten children born to Dr. Ramon Granados Marquez and Maria de la Concepcion Rey Capdevilla, a Spanish couple that immigrated to the U. S. in 1911. After living at several locations in the Washington D. C. area, they rented in 1917 and later purchased a large Victorian house in Riverdale, MD. That same year they became naturalized citizens.

In 1937 the household consisted of Ramon, the father (known to me as *Abuelo*), three youngest

Granados children; Juan (Johnny) 19, Mercedes (Beano), 17 and Tony, 15. The mother Maria died in 1932. In June 1937 my mother, Clara Granados Koch, the fourth Granados child, went to the hospital to give birth to my sister Barbara. My older by almost two years sister, "little Clara" and I stayed in the Victorian house under the care of *Abuelo* and the three youngest Granados. Quite unexpectedly that afternoon, Dr. Ramon Granados Marques 56 (Abuelo) died in his office of a paralytic stroke.

The occupants of the Riverdale Victorian house were moved out to make room for Luis Granados, the oldest son, and his family that inherited the house. Clara and I returned to our own house with Beano. Johnny and Tony went to live with their older brother Ramon and his wife Kitty until Tony graduated from Hyattsville High School.

Ramon and Kitty lived just a few blocks from our house and thus there were many opportunities for interactions with Tony. I have few memories of those days because I was only five, but Tony often mentioned walking to movies with my father and standing on the grate of the whole house furnace to warm up.

After graduating high school Tony worked in DC for several years, then moved to Philadelphia, PA to work until he became a US Marine Corp pilot in 1944. I next saw Tony briefly in 1945 when he came to Riverdale Heights to visit Ramon and Kitty before picking up his life after the war. He returned to the

Philadelphia area, married his sweetheart Rita, entered Wharton School of Finance and Commerce and began his family. He was called back to duty during the Korean War in 1951. By that time he had graduated college, started a business and had three children.

I joined the Marine Corp in 1951 and spent three years as an electronics instructor at the Naval Air Technical Training Center in Millington, TN. Tony however, was in the thick of the fighting in Korea. Tony flew 82 missions and returned home in June, 1952 having been awarded two Distinguished Flying Crosses, four air metals and assorted campaign ribbons. While in Korea, he was so concerned about the poorly clothed Korean children in an orphanage near his base that he arranged a clothing drive in his home town to collect used clothing for the orphans. One ton of clothes reached the orphanage due to the generosity of people in his home area of Pennsylvania.

The squadron that he flew in had a distinctive checkerboard pattern painted on the cowling and when Tony's wife saw a picture in the newspaper of a plane with a checkerboard cowling that had crashed on a carrier deck she wrote telling him to be careful. Turns out that it was his plane and he considered himself the luckiest man to serve in Korea. Good luck seemed to follow Granados men. His brother Johnny once stepped off of the fifth floor roof of a building only to be caught by a painter on a ladder at the third floor!

Tony and I lived our separate lives and I did not see him again until the first Granados reunion picnic in 1970. I would only see Tony, from time to time, at the reunions. When I retired I moved from Norfolk, VA, where I taught geology at the Old Dominion University, to Annapolis, MD to be close to my mother. She was in poor health and living in Deale Beach, about 25 miles south of Annapolis. None of my three siblings lived in the area so I took care of her financial and physical well being. When she could no longer attend the Granados family reunions, Tony would occasionally visit her at her house. Tony and I became better acquainted during those times.

On one occasion in the early 2000s he drove from Pennsylvania to my Annapolis home to visit Annapolis and to get better acquainted. That night I cooked chicken and sausage gumbo for dinner. The secret to this dish and other Cajun dishes is the roux. Most recipes start "first you make a roux", for which equal parts of flour and fat are cooked over high heat until the mixture is a very dark brown. Tony's curiosity about all things meant that he watched intently as the roux was being made.

The next day my wife Joyce, Tony and I visited the Naval Academy. At the gate we were barred entry because Joyce had no I.D. Not a problem, Tony opened his wallet showing that he was still a member of the Marine Corp reserves and I think his rank was Lt. Colonel. Tony wanted to see the Chapel and the museum. The large chapel is a solemn place dedicated to the men that have died in battle. A wedding was taking place there that day.

The museum had many items from past Naval actions. It was in the museum that Tony told me about the hierarchy within the Navy which he referred to as the black shoe navy and the brown shoe navy. The black shoe navy is the old Navy of battleships and cruisers. The black shoe people consider that they represent the real Navy. I mused to myself about John McCain whose father and grandfathers were Admirals. How did that work out for him as a Naval aviator?

After my mother was gone and I could no longer manage to maintain a house and garden, Joyce and I moved to a Continuous Care Retirement Community (CCRC) in Mitchellville, MD where the yards and building maintenance are provided. Also provided is one meal a day removing the necessity of cooking.

Cooking had been my favorite activity, thus at the CCRC I had time on my hands. I started taking courses in memoir writing and managed to write a number of one or two page papers mostly on episodes during my life. I sent Tony several of the earliest papers about a year ago. I believe he enjoyed them and he replied that it had been a simpler time when happiness was "a bushel of hard crabs and screens on the windows". After five semesters I had written 33 papers and had them bound. These bound collections were sent to my siblings and several close friends.

This past July I sent the collection of papers to Tony believing that he would enjoy some of them. He wrote back and said "I read them in two sittings. They were easy to read, since I knew many of the characters and places. For me, personally they were even more interesting for the same reasons". He went on to mention fur trapping, Greenbelt and my father's life-long love of tennis. Additionally he wrote "I am in awe of your academic accomplishments and am very proud to call you Doctor". Obviously he had missed many of my activities that he only learned about through my memoirs. My mind boggles at the thought of how much of his life I had similarly missed.

For example, I never met his wife, Rita. A nurse, she died in an automobile accident returning home on a snowy night after working the hospital night shift. She was 56. I met three of his six children for the first time at the viewing. They were terrific people – Rosemary was a retired labor judge, John, a retired dentist like his maternal grandfather and Lizz works at Pennsylvania University as a computer lecturer. The remaining three of Tony's children remain unmet. I truly regret that I totally missed knowing Tony's family.

In fact, of my 43 first cousins, I have met only 16. I am saddened to think of how interesting these people must have been. Most of them still are. During my two careers, electronics engineer and Geology professor, I was focused, worked hard, and therefore in my own mind successful. I didn't stop and "smell the roses". This I regret.

Later I learned that the papers were read to him by his daughter Mary and his reply dictated to his daughter Lizz. He was near the end when he "read" my 33 papers and I am so very pleased to have brought him some joy.

Tony had been instrumental in planning the family reunions, the creation of a family website, genealogy investigation of the family history and generally facilitating relationships within the family. For me and the other 43 second generation family members he was our beloved "Uncle Tony".

Starting as an orphan at 15, through intelligences and strength of character, tony lived the "American Dream". Wonderful father of 6, successful businessman, patriot, giving of himself through this life are some of his attributes. He leaves this world better than he found it.

The House on
Charlotte Avenue

I N THE EARLY 1930's my parents purchased a small
house on Charlotte Avenue in Riverdale Heights,
Maryland, an unincorporated community of 600-
700 persons, 2 churches (Lutheran and Baptist), a
grocery store and a volunteer fire department.
Charlotte Avenue was a black top county road that
ran the length of the community. From the road,
this small house could be seen as a wood frame, one
story building having an attic with a small dormer,
full basement and a porch across the front. There
was a driveway on the right side, vacant lots on
either side, two snowball bushes in the front yard
and a barberry hedge.

The house had two bedrooms, bath, kitchen, dining room and living room. My sister Clara and I occupied the front bedroom and the parents the back one. The living room had a large grate that provided heat to the whole house, upright piano, radio, Victrola, couch and two chairs. The front bedroom had a closet that included a ladder to the attic. In the back bedroom a chifferobe served as the closet.

The bathroom included a tub on feet, toilet, wash basin and running water. In the kitchen were a gas stove, refrigerator, sink and an oil cloth covered breakfast table with four chairs. The door to the screened back porch was located here. The dining room contained a table and chairs, buffet, china closet, bookcase and a door to the unfinished full basement.

In the back yard were a victory garden, scientifically designed chicken coop for laying hens and a small creek. Caring for the chickens was my job and included feeding, cleaning and collecting eggs. I relished the fact that the chickens and I had to answer to no one else when we were in the coop.

Many of my fondest memories occurred in the living room. When I returned home from school I would listen to radio shows such as Jack Armstrong, All American Boy or the Green Hornet. After dinner my mother, sister Clara and I would listen to such shows as Amos and Andy, Duffy's Tavern, Jack Benny, Judy Canova and Lux Radio Theater.

Occasionally this would include a few candy bars such as Baby Ruth, Butterfinger or Milky Way which were obtained by a quick run (by me) to the store. Sometimes Clara and I would listen to the Victrola and the vinyl records from the 20's and 30's.

When I was eight years of age I stayed home from school one day with a cold. While recuperating on the couch in the living room I came across some envelopes with postage stamps. That was the beginning of a lifelong hobby of stamp collecting and I still have several boxes and albums of stamps.

Of my childhood memories none were more beautiful than those of Christmas. On Christmas Eve, Santa came while Clara and I were asleep. In the morning where the couch had been in the living room was a beautiful Christmas tree decked out with abundant bulbs, lights, sparkly garland and shiny tinsel. The tree stand was a garden surrounded by a picket fence, crafted by my grandfather, with miniature people and animals on snow. To a child, it was a miracle that Santa could do these things in such a short period of time and the first sight was nearly overwhelming.

My first 14 years were spent in the house on Charlotte Avenue in the suburbs of Washington, D.C. It should be obvious to all that I greatly enjoyed those experiences.

The Chicken Coop

THE CHICKEN COOP was a private sanctuary for me—just me and the chickens! There were a variety of smells, some pleasant, some more pungent. Straw was the smell when the floor litter was replaced. As part of a bale was pulled apart, the odor of fresh straw was released. The chicken had a unique smell of a warm body, feathers and feet. And of course, their roost smelled of chicken manure.

These chickens were egg layers and therefore were fed a mash. In the winter, I would pour hot water into a bowl of mash to encourage the hens to feed. The hot, steaming mash exuded its own smell. When one entered the coop in early morning after the door had been shut all night against the cold, the overall smell depended on factors such as time of last straw replacement, when the roost had been cleaned and how many chickens were there. It was always a pleasant smell to me.

The Gum Tree

BEFORE THE ADVENT of television, what did young children do to amuse themselves on long summer days? For me it was playing in the dirt with little cars. My favorite place was at the base of a large gum tree that stood alone at the corner of two intersecting roads. The tree sat way back from the streets such as to provide ample space of unvegetated dirt, some of which was loose enough to dig little roads and little garages. The tree provided shade and a slight breeze was usually present. Tommy Swindell, a neighbor boy about my age, and I would while away hours at a time digging in the dirt and playing with little cars. In the days before air conditioning and television, we were never bored or hot.

Hurrahs for the
Volunteer Firemen

RIVERDALE HEIGHTS WAS an unincorporated working class community at the end of the city bus line where Washington, D.C. met rural Maryland. Most of the men worked in D.C. for private companies and most had moved to Riverdale Heights for less expensive housing. None of these men were drafted during World War II either because they were too old or because they had too many children.

Most wholeheartedly supported the volunteer fire department by answering the siren in the middle of the night or helping to raise funds for equipment or operating expenses or both. The fire department provided protection against fires and offered an opportunity for service to the community. I remember that my father had boots and fireman's clothing next to his bed. When the siren went off he would quickly dress and dash the two blocks to the fire house. The volunteer fire department also served as the most important social and cultural binding force. There was no dominate religion, employer or ethnicity.

Not all of the residents of Riverdale Heights joined in the activities of the volunteer fire department. I do not know about about those residents that did not participate but I can describe the firemen well. They were mostly craftsmen such as carpenters, bricklayers, plumbers, printers, plasterers and auto mechanics. One was a driver for Wonder Bread who also was elected head of the drivers' union. He was also the fire chief for many years, a strong leader and my uncle. None were college graduates, few were high school graduates. Their origins were, for the most part, western and southern Europe. Some were born in Europe or born to recent immigrants and some were of origins blurred by time but with Anglo-Saxon names. There were no African Americans, Asian Americans, Latinos, Muslims and only one Jewish family that ran the grocery store. Most were protestants but many were Catholics.

Funds were raised in several ways. Once a year, the fire trucks would drive the streets and firemen would solicit money from the homeowners. In the summer each year the firemen would host one of the traveling carnivals for a week providing labor to prepare the grounds and man the booths. As a climax "Dare Devil Oliver" would dive off a high tower into a miniscule tank. Many of the wives joined the woman's auxiliary and as a group would occasionally have bake sales.

By far, my favorite fund raisers were the several oyster roasts held during the coldest months. Men from far around would come for oysters, beer and poker. One of the Riverdale Heights firemen was reputed to make the best oyster stew in the region. I worked outdoors roasting oysters. A large pit with a hot wood fire was covered by a steel plate. Oysters were spread on the plate and covered with soaking wet burlap bags. When the burlap was dry, the oysters were cooked. I loved to take the finished product into the kitchen because then I could grab a handful of pretzels before returning to duty at the fire.

Although I have no solid data, my guess is that the most money was raised at the poker tables. A fireman dealt the cards for each of the 4-6 tables. If the pot was small, the dealer would drag a chip or two for the house. If the pot was large, the house took a larger share. Men who win large pots can be very generous and never objected.

Prince George's County honored its volunteer firemen with a picnic each year at Magruder Park in Hyattsville. Competition between the firemen of the different departments included softball games and tug-o-war. Great fun was had in the Prince George's County suburbs of Washington D.C. It was the 1930s and 40s and I was a child, and then I wasn't.

The Tennis Player

MY FATHER WAS a union printer who loved to play tennis. His early heroes were big Bill Tilden and Don Budge, the champions of the 1920s and 1930s respectively. It was not easy for a blue collar worker of limited resources to find a venue in which to play. There were no Departments of Recreation or public courts sponsored by the county, state or federal government.

He played tennis before 1937 but I was too young to know where he found courts. In 1937 he was one of the founders of the Witintide Tennis Club near Tuxedo, MD, that used a court owned by one Edward M. Horman. Mr. Horman owned about 100 acres of flat land adjacent to the Anacostia River and just within the D.C. Line on the same side and downstream from Bladensburg, MD. The court was well removed from the house such that the members could play without disturbing Mr. Horman. The Witentide Tennis Club constitution limited membership to 20 men, required dues of one dollar per month and listed "the object of the organization to encourage better tennis playing in the broadest and most liberal manner". The men who played on Mr. Horman's court felt that they should manage and maintain the clay courts so that Mr. Horman did not have that expense.

Shortly after 1937, at the age of five, I began to accompany my father every time he played. Each weekend and several times a week during the longer summer days we went to the court. Upon arriving the routine was as follows: first the court was rolled with a very heavy water filled roller, then a large rug was dragged across the surface to smooth the clay, then lines were made using a liquid mixture of water and lime. This was a joint effort by the players. When the lines were dry, play began.

During play, I just hung out, climbing trees, investigating the fields and woods and occasionally running errands. During hot weather I was sent to a cool natural spring in the woods to get a mason jar full of water – sometimes I was given a dime.

My father's love of the sport knew no bounds. One July day, the match went on for a long time. In those days, tie breakers did not exist. Finally, the winning set was over 22-20. When my father and I arrived home I learned that my mother had a birthday party for me but by then everyone had gone home. My father knew of the planned party but was compelled to keep playing.

On another occasion we stopped at a small airport located near the tennis court to see why there was a crowd and we learned that the famous aviator Clarence Chamberlin was barnstorming. Clarence Chamberlin was famous as the second man to pilot a fixed-wing aircraft across the Atlantic Ocean, from New York to the European mainland while carrying the first transatlantic passenger in 1933. He was taking people up for a little fly around for money in the famous airplane. When we got there, there was one seat left and no takers. My father offered them fifty cents to take me and they accepted. I remember flying over the Potomac River and seeing people on the ice of a frozen river. On that extremely cold day, my father had tried to play tennis, maybe he actually did.

He continued to play tennis until he was 87 or 88. He died at 89. Towards the end while in his eighties he delighted in beating the young 60 year old opponents. Public television did a program on athletes still playing into their 80s and my father was the feature for a tennis player. He was "A Tennis Player".

Hyattsville in My Youth

OOKING OUT A big picture window while lunching at Franklin's Restaurant in Hyattsville I noticed the old National Guard Armory a few blocks north on Route 1. This building, with its distinctive turrets now painted white over the original stone, brought back hundreds of memories of the Hyattsville of my youth during the 40s and 50s.

At that time Hyattsville was the commercial and cultural center of the northern half of Prince George's County and the majority of county residents lived in the northern half. Access to Washington DC was easy by the streetcar, B & O railroad, Route 1 and Rhode Island Avenue. Until the local building boom of the 50s and the opening of the super mall Prince George's Plaza, people in the area depended on

Hyattsville for shopping, movies and the important services available at the County Service Building.

Important to me was the Hyattsville Hardware Store that sold tools, nails in bulk, hunting equipment and miscellaneous hardware. Franklin's Restaurant is housed next to the original building. I bought my first shotgun there at age 14, a used Harrington and Richardson single shot 20 gauge and the following year a dozen bright and shiny Oneida muskrat traps. When a customer bought nails they went to rotating bins filled with nails of various sizes and shapes, used a big scoop, put the nails on the scale and when they had the right amount, emptied the scale tray into a small brown paper bag. They then took the bag to the cashier, told him the contents and he rang up that amount without checking. It was the honor system that is now perhaps a thing of the past.

Those same nail bins are now filled with small Mary Janes and other candies, sold by the pound. Franklin's has turned the old hardware part of the building into a country store selling chili sauces, wine, gag gifts and cards, weird books, earrings, etc.

The building next door, now demolished, housed the bowling alley. Ten pin bowling was unknown locally until the 60s. Before then duckpins were the bowling of choice. Duck pin uses a smaller ball without holes and smaller pins. A strike is rare and an average above 100 was unusual. The volunteer firemen had a league where fire departments competed every Tuesday night. The pins were set by boys that perched above and dropped down after the ball was rolled to set the pins Sometimes flying pins would even hit the boys, and they were only paid a paltry sum of $.10 a line.

Opposite the armory was the Hot Shoppe where high school students went after the games for tasty barbeque, french fries, and either a chocolate shake or an orange freeze.

The next block north on Route 1 was a row of shops including High's Ice Cream, Woolworth's 5 and dime and Pep Boys for auto supplies.

At the top of the hill was a new movie theater, Sidney Lust's Hyattsville Cinema. We went there for the Saturday matinee which usually included a double feature, three comedies such as Our Gang or the Three Stooges or animated cartoons such as Popeye or Bugs Bunny and a serial that continued from week to week. The price was 15 cents.

When my mother returned to the work force she worked at High's serving ice cream and later Woolworth's. Prince George's Plaza opened in 1959 and she worked the hosiery counter at Hecht's where she could keep an eye on the entrance. She knew many the people that entered and some of them were relatives.

One block from Franklin's was Boswell Burke Heating and Air Conditioning. I worked there for two summers while in high school.

On my 16th birthday I drove my '37 Ford to work and during lunch time drove the two blocks to the

County Service Building, passed the driving test and went back to work. The County Service Building is also where I enlisted in the Marine Corps one month before my 18th birthday.

On Rhode Island Avenue several blocks towards DC was the Marché's Florist. During the high school years everyone bought corsages for their prom date there – usually a gardenia or a camellia. Orchids were too pricy. I think they were $11.

Hyattsville played an important role in my life before I was eighteen. I bought my first shotgun, rolled my first duck pin line, snacked at the Hot Shoppe, attended the Saturday matinee, bought prom corsages, enlisted in the Marine Corp, worked two summers and obtained my driver's license in Hyattsville. There are many other firsts that happened in that town and my memories are vivid and priceless.

Going Downtown

I GREW UP in an unincorporated area east of Riverdale (now Riverdale Park) with a population of 600 to 700. This was during the 30s and 40s. A small grocery store run by Archie and Henrietta Rosenblatz was the only shopping available. All other shopping was in downtown Washington DC. We could take public transportation,

I was ten years old the first time I went to downtown alone and I had no qualms about getting lost. The money in my pocket was earned babysitting. It amuses me that there are now laws to prevent babysitting at such an early age. Maryland law requires 13 years and Illinois law requires that children under 14 cannot be left unattended.

The end of the line from the District of Columbia (DC) was located at the junction of Riverdale Road and Kenilworth Avenue. Both were two lane blacktop roads at that time. Across Riverdale Road were pastures of Browning's Dairy and nearby was Saint John's Evangelical Lutheran Church where I attended Sunday School and earned a medal for six years of perfect attendance.

The bus labeled "East Riverdale" waited there at the end of the line until it was time to leave. A six block walk from my house and I could get on the bus. The bus traveled past the Peace Cross and the iconic Bar B Que joint and honkytonk called the Dixie Pig to Mt. Ranier. Once I went by the Peace Cross area which often flooded and all that remained of the Dixie Pig was the lower three feet of the wall. The Dixie Pig had caught fire during a flood and firemen could not reach it. The Corps of Engineers has since built levees to prevent flooding.

The street car came to Mt. Ranier and using a transfer you received upon boarding the bus you then boarded the street car to NW Washington.

The street car ran along Rhode Island Avenue and at the District line you could see on the left Fleishman's Yeast Factory which I thought was unique was in fact one of hundreds worldwide and Jimmy La Fontaine's Gambling Palace.

Jimmy LaFontaine's Gambling Palace was high class with formal attire required. It was located in Maryland because the laws were looser than in DC.

It was the largest gambling establishment between Schenectady, New York and Florida.

The street car then passed in front of McKinley Tech the premier High School in the district. It looked like a huge mansion at a time when I attended Bladensburg High School near the Peace Cross which was the size of a present day grammar school. Then the streetcar turned onto G St. NW about where Chinatown began. We passed parallel to Chinatown which was six or eight blocks long in those days. Chinatown had several thousand inhabitants then compared to several hundred today.

On G St. at 7th was the original Hecht's, a department store. Hecht's has since been bought by Macy's. Large purchases from Hecht's such as stoves or refrigerators were picked up at the warehouse on New York Avenue. The Hecht's Warehouse has recently been converted to condominium apartments and small shops.

From 7th St. to 15th St. the trolly traveled on G St., a short block away from F St. At about 12th was Woodward and Lothrup, an upscale department store. They had the best window displays at Christmas and a Stamp Shop. I would always go past the stamp shop to see the philatelic material that was sure to be way beyond my price range.

There were three 5 and dime stores: Woolworth's, Murphy's and a new one that opened in about 1948 named McCrory's. The merchandise was not expensive and they were good places to buy underwear and socks. Murphy's had a large pet store with goldfish, guppies, turtles, Salamanders and fancy tropical fish. My mother bought me an angel fish and on other occasions I bought a salamander and a small turtle. I was disdainful of goldfish because you had to change the water each day.

At 14th and 15th were Garfinkles and Jellefs, upscale shops for women's clothes. Along the seven blocks of F St. between 7th and 15th there were six movie houses, two of which had stage shows with vaudeville acts.

At about 11th St. was a nut shop which smelled wonderful when you walked past. I would sometimes buy a small amount of broken cashews. I loved cashews but could not afford the best ones. There was also a beggar who had apparently lost his legs and he would grind his organ. His pet rhesus monkey would hold out a cup for donations. After a couple of hours walking along F St. it was back to G Street to catch the "Mt. Ranier Streetcar" and then the "East Riverdale" bus and a short walk home

When malls were built in the 50s patronage along 7th Street declined slowly and after the riots over the assassination of Martin Luther King some suburbanites were afraid to go to the District. F St. ceased to be the shopping mecca for the Washington DC area.

Insert The 8th Grade

I N THE 1940s Prince George's County was mostly a rural area with much of the population clustered close to the northeast boundary with Washington, DC. The county service building was in Hyattsville, central to this most populated area but the County Seat was in Upper Marlboro in the more geographic center of the county. In what was apparently a surprise move by the legislators, they mandated that the school board increase the number of years of public school from 11 to 12 years. This change was to begin fall 1946 and I was in the first class under the new plan.

The school board was caught off guard because they had not known that the change was coming and therefore had to quickly develop curricula and arrange for classrooms. In the past, elementary school was seven grades and high school was four, there were no middle schools.

The question was how and where to locate the additional year. The solution selected was to insert the 8th grade at the beginning of high school.

There were advantages to being the first class to attend 12 years. Of course we benefited from the additional year of classes. In addition, during our last two years we were essentially the senior class. We acted in the plays, wrote the newspaper and yearbook, populated the National Honor Society and had leading roles on the sports teams. This aided in our process of maturing and provided valuable experience in managing a variety of activities.

The graduating class of 1950 numbered 184 and included no African Americans, Latinos, Asian Americans, or Muslims. It did include Alan Klawans, who was Jewish. Most of these students had working class fathers and stay at home moms. Some lived in the towns bordering Washington, DC such as Colmar Manor, Cottage City, Tuxedo and Beaver Creek. Others students were from the nearby small rural farms in areas such as Glendale and Wildercroft. High schools surrounding Bladensburg High School were in Greenbelt, Hyattsville, Mt. Rainier and Suitland.

For many years some students from Prince George's County attended high school in Washington DC to obtain a better education. In 1949, the District of Columbia imposed tuition on those students not actually living in Washington. Most could not afford the tuition and therefore some attended Bladensburg High School for our senior year. One of these students was Filipino, thus doubling our diversity and his name was Paul Magtutu. Also in 1949, football was introduced to the Prince George's County High Schools. Prior to that year the major winter sport was soccer. Bladensburg High School won the county championship the first year, perhaps because we inherited three experienced players who had previously played for Eastern High School in nearby Washington D.C. They were the previously mentioned Paul Magtutu, a quarterback, and his two large cousins the Medina brothers who were offensive linemen. Another outstanding player was Jackie Davis from my neighborhood, Riverdale Heights. Jackie went on to play for Fort Bragg, the University of Maryland and briefly with the Redskins. Paul Magtutu also played for the University of Maryland but not in a starting role.

My friend, Ronnie Willoner and I were made team managers. That summer I was sent to the University of Maryland to learn trainer stuff under the then well known Maryland trainer Duke Wire. Trainer stuff included such tasks as bandaging injuries and taping ankles. During games Ronnie handled the water and towels and I handled the taping and injuries.

I do not know the subsequent history of most of these 184 persons. I do know, however that at the 50th reunion we were asked how many had served in the military. Every male hand went up, indicating that all had served their country in the time of need, particularly during the Korean War. About half of the class seems to have migrated to The Villages in Central Florida and these people occasionally hold mini class reunions there.

I know more detail about the lives of several classmates and I am impressed with their accomplishments. Paul Magtutu was an Air Force Colonel at the time of the 50th reunion. Jackie Davis used his local fame to be a TV commentator, wrestling referee and in the service of Catholic Charities. Alan Klawan is a well respected graphic artist in Philadelphia. Ronnie Willoner is a well known local lawyer who has yet to retire at 82 due to dedication to his clients' needs. Before retirement I gained some international recognition among paleontologists for my pioneering work on quantitative analysis of the fossil records. Others were teachers in high schools and colleges which I attribute to the Bladensburg High School teachers that were such good role models. I know of at least two that went on to become college presidents.

It should be obvious to the reader that I cherish the memories, love my classmates and respect the lives they lived. We followed closely on the heels of the "greatest generation."

Growing Up Near Greenbelt

A N HISTORIC PLANNED community exists about seven miles north of Collington. It was one of three built during the Roosevelt administration that were noted for their interior walkways, underpasses and some of the first mall-type shopping centers in the US. The other two were in Wisconsin and Ohio.

This community was near my childhood home and touched my life several times. The first was in 1937 when FDR came to dedicate the community. He traveled from the White House to Greenbelt (about 10 miles) along Kenilworth Avenue. My mother took me the several blocks from our house to Kenilworth Avenue. I saw FDR ride by in an open car.

The architecture was streamlined in the Art Deco style popular at that time and some of the original buildings are considered among the best examples of Art Deco presently in the US. In 1939 the swimming pool opened and it was the first public swimming pool in the Washington area. I remember making my way to swim for the first time and many times in the absence of direct public transportation. It required a one mile walk to the streetcar in Riverdale that terminated in Beltsville. At Beltsville we took a bus to Greenbelt ending a 2 hour odyssey. Of course we had to come back.

Greenbelt was also a social experiment. Designed to provide low income housing, it drew 5700 applicants for the original 885 residences. In 1941 another 1000 homes were added to provide housing for families coming to Washington in connection with defense programs of World War II. By 1954, when I was discharged from the Marine Corps, these 1000 newer units had become veteran's housing primarily for students at the University of Maryland. I qualified on both counts.

This housing consisted of a number of frame buildings that looked like large army barracks. Each building was divided into ten one bedroom apartments. The price was right. My little family of three rented one for $49.50. I graduated from the university and this apartment three years later.

Those years encompassed the McCarthy hearings. The Republican senator (a former marine) from Wisconsin, Joe McCarthy, claimed that there were hundreds of communists in the State Department undermining our government during the Cold War. He then orchestrated a committee to sort out the commies. Many of the residents of Greenbelt were progressive and had been attracted by the social experiment of the planned community. A few had been members of the communist party in the early 30s or knew someone that had been. That was all the evidence that Joe McCarthy needed to brand such people as the enemy. Several of these people lost their government jobs at this time and could not find other employment.

Over the years, Greenbelt expanded to include additional developed areas nearby. In 1959 NASA's World and Space Flight Center opened on a nearby spot that I have always considered the best squirrel hunting location of my youth. The present population of Greenbelt is about 24,000 and the core area still operates in the original cooperative manner. The Baltimore-Washington Parkway opened in the early 50s and in the 70s the capital beltway (I-495/95). In addition Kenilworth Avenue was straightened and widened. These three important roads meet in Greenbelt and the city has become a major commercial center in Prince George's County.

Respect for Nature

I T WAS LATE 1945, the war was over, Christmas was fast approaching and I was fourteen. I told my father that I wanted a 22 caliber rifle to hunt. To this he replied, "you don't want a rifle to hunt with, you want a shotgun". Alright then, I wanted a shotgun! Guns were not generally available because of the war, but we somehow learned that the owner of the Hyattsville Hardware Store had a shotgun for sale. For $15 we bought a used Harrington and Richardson single shot 20 gauge shotgun as a Christmas present for me.

The next weekend my father took me to some open land on the left bank of the Anacostia River between Bladensburg and the Kenilworth Gardens to teach me about shotguns. I barely got to touch the gun.

My father loved the outdoors and since he no longer had the wartime "civil defense" responsibilities he had time for recreation. Thus began five years in which the two of us hunted, fished and trapped every chance we got.

During the various hunting seasons starting with doves, then squirrels, then rabbits and quail and finally ducks and geese, we hunted something every Saturday until early January. When the weather allowed and the hunting season had not yet started, we fished. Most often we caught bass, blue gills and crappie at the Tridelphia and Rocky Gorge Reservoirs in Montgomery and Howard Counties. The trapping season for muskrats and mink took place between January 1 and March 15, a time when fishing and hunting were out of season. No problem. We got up at 4:00 am every morning to check the traps before sunup so that no one could observe where our traps were set. And yes, some mornings were very cold. The activity truly tested our love of the outdoors.

The coldest weather that I ever experienced, however, was the time that we went to Pocomoke State Park in Worchester County to hunt deer in early December. The temperature that night dropped to a very uncommon 10 F. We tried sleeping on Army cots in a pup tent but we were not able to sleep that night. This was before sleeping bags were commonly available but sleeping bags undoubtedly would have made sleep possible.

Our respect for nature meant that we never killed a bird, fish or animal that we could not use. For example, we never shot blackbirds for target practice as others were known to do. This just never seemed right to us. When trapping we occasionally caught an opossum, an animal whose fur brought between five and twenty-five cents at the raw fur market. To see that this animal's life was respected, we skinned it, dried the pelt and mailed it off to receive a token amount of money. We never caught more fish than we could eat. Our motto was that if you kill it, you eat it or at least see that it serves some purpose.

After I enlisted in the Marine Corp, my father continued those outdoor activities. He especially liked the Pocomoke State Park. The Pokomoke River is amazing in that it is very deep for its width and large vessels were able to reach Snow Hill, about 20 miles up river from the Chesapeake Bay. The water is black and the shores are lined with Cyprus trees. It is more like a river in Florida than one in Maryland. He also took my mother and their grandchildren camping there in the summer months.

The warden was so impressed with my father's love of the outdoors, that he told him about a two and a half acre, privately owned, property within the park itself. The warden thought it was available for purchase. The property belonged to a church congregation that had planned to build a church, thus the state did not buy the land when it established the park. However, the park encompassed such a wide area, in which so few people lived, that the congregation could not justify building a new church. After several years of indecision the church members sold the two and one half acres to my father for about $200. Later I helped my father move a small used camping trailer, that he bought cheap, from Hyattsville to the Pocomoke property. It was no mean feat to move a very rickety trailer cautiously for 100 miles.

One later squirrel hunting season we took my uncle Johnny to introduce him to hunting. He had not spent much of his life off of the pavement except for two years in North Africa with the U.S. Army during World War II. We slept in the trailer so that we could hunt early the next day. Early that next morning we split up to hunt individually, planning to assemble mid-day at the trailer for lunch. Each of us had shot some squirrels, however, Johnny's one squirrel was actually a ground squirrel better known as a chipmunk.

As our motto, "you kill it you eat it", meant the chipmunk had to be eaten. Grey squirrels are delicious but a chipmunk's taste was an unknown. Johnny had been a chef/cook for Ceres Restaurant at 12th and E St. NW for 20 years and that next night brought to our house a sauteed chipmunk in a sherry and green olive sauce. We all ate some. It was pretty good with the sauce and excellent preparation. This was a "memorable meal" not only because it was tasty (although meager) but also because it was a testimonial to our respect for nature.

When my father died in 1998, I was the executor of his estate. I had always felt that the Pocomoke land was actually part of the park and had been wrongly acquired by my father. It would be a shame if some mansion was built upon it. The property must be become part of the Pocomoke State Forest. My lawyer, Ron Willoner, suggested that we offer it to the state at one half of the appraised value. This was acceptable after the state comptroller drove to Worchester County and saw the property. It was done. The two and one half acres are now part of Pocomoke State Park.

That comptroller was William Shaeffer, age 80. He is an example of a truly dedicated public servant, having served the City of Baltimore and the state of Maryland for over fifty two years. He sat on the city council at 34, was Mayor of Baltimore at 50, Governor from 66 to 74, and comptroller from age 78 to 86. He spent his entire life in service to his community. My respect for William Shaeffer increased because he drove to the Pokomoke State Park over a very small amount of money to make sure that it was a fair deal for Maryland.

When he ceased to be governor, he retired. The opportunity to be comptroller came up after Louis Goldstein died. Louis Goldstein was comptroller of Maryland for 40 years, making him the longest serving state official in US history. When he died in 1998, William Shaeffer ran for the office of comptroller and won. Obviously he liked to stay busy.

I have been blessed that so much of my life has been spent outdoors. The deep respect that I have for nature came from within me and not from these outdoor experiences. It never made sense to take more from nature than necessary. Skinning an opossum, drying its pelts and mailing it to a raw fur market for a nickle was out of respect for the opossum's life. Preparing a chipmunk dinner with great care and joining in eating the animal attests to Uncle Johnny's respect for nature. Making sure that Pocomoke State Forest remains all park and no houses by selling the two and one half acre property to the state of Maryland at a bargain price was one way that I showed my respect. If enough people act in a similar manner our planet will go on forever.

Let's hope so.

Muskrats and Me

MY FIRST ENCOUNTER with muskrats occurred in the late 40s when my father and I trapped fur-bearing animals along the creeks in College Park, Maryland. During a four year period we caught about 100 muskrats, 12 mink, 8 racoons, 6 opossums, 2 foxes, 2 skunk and 1 weasel. All the furs were scraped, stretched and dried. The dried furs were mailed to the Sears, Roebuck raw fur market in New Jersey. Sears knew that the money paid for the fur would come back to them from catalog sales. The only furs worth much were the mink (about $10 each) and muskrats ($2-3 each). The other furs were virtually worthless ($.50 or less), but we sent them off to honor our commitment to not harvest wildlife without a purpose.

My father knew exactly how to catch muskrats. He grew up in Washington, D. C.'s Congress Heights and a few blocks from the Congressional Cemetery. If one continues east a small distance beyond the cemetery they will encounter the right bank of the Anacostia River. In the first few decades of the twentieth century the river was clear and faster moving. This is hard to imagine one hundred years later with its mud laden water and slow tidal flow that has resulted from housing development in Prince George's and Montgomery Counties. How my father learned about trapping is not known by me but it might have been an older brother, neighbor or one of those unattached men who lived in a very small shack along the river and made a meager living by fishing. In any event, it was along the Anacostia River that my father developed a strong love of outdoor activities like hunting, fishing and trapping.

He passed this love of the outdoors to me. In my teens, we hunted together during hunting season, fished together the rest of the year and when fishing was a poor or even fruitless at times during the trapping season, we trapped together. Any activity that required spending the day in the field or on the water, no matter the weather, we undertook. Trapping was that activity for January, February and the first half of March. We did not trap for money but rather sold the furs to honor our pact with Mother Nature.

The name muskrat is unfortunate. Instead of thinking of something undesirable or threatening, think of a small beaver. Its fur is soft and thick giving the muskrat a cuddly appearance. The tail is not round but flattened in the vertical plane and used by the muskrat for sculling. The two musk glands have a sweet smell not unlike a very expensive perfume and is in fact used as a base for many perfumes. Muskrat fur constitutes the majority of fur used in garments worldwide because of its warmth and flexibility. Many people in rural Maryland and other places consider muskrats as "good eats".

Since my trapping muskrat days I have lived an exciting life and I now live in a continuing care facility that has a beautiful lake. The lake serves as my motivation when I walk daily for my health. At the lake are sometimes found interesting wildlife. Ducks and geese, herons and kingfisher, blue birds and bald eagles have been seen there by me. During early January I witnessed a muskrat carrying nesting material to a location under the pier. The animal worked constantly for a few days and eventually completed the nest. After that, I only saw the muskrat once every several days. A few weeks ago we had a light snow that settled on the ice at the pier. That morning I looked down and saw a perfect set of mink tracks. Mink are the major predators of muskrats and when I didn't see the muskrat for over a week I feared the worst. This morning I saw the muskrat again and I was joyful.

The Patuxent River in My Life and Beyond

THE PATUXENT RIVER has been the site of some interesting events in my life over the past eight decades. Events range from fishing in Tridelphia Reservoir in the north downriver a hundred miles to the Calvert Marine Museum near Solomons Island.

When I was eleven years old my parents rented a tiny frame cottage from a friend near Benedict on the Patuxent River. During that week I watched a neighbor, Mr. Hausemann return with his catch from a pound net he had offshore. The catch included fish species of commercial value which he sold and some that he returned to the river.

Later I found a twelve foot minnow seine at the cottage and by forcing one pole into the bottom and dragging the seine in a semicircle caught the animals that lived at the shore line. This included all manner of marine life such as silver-sided minnows, small blue crabs, grass shrimp, jellyfish, seaweed and shells. These fascinated me and I became a lover of water living animals and fished or crabbed somewhere for the next fifty years.

When I was about five, the James family moved into a house just two doors down. The family consisted of Father James, an Episcopal priest from Peoria, Illinois, who had been assigned to the Church of the Epiphany on G street NW, in Washington, DC. and his wife Vinnie. She had left three grandsons in Peoria, Illinois so I became the recipient of many homemade sugar cookies as their proxy. A single daughter, Janet, worked in the church business office and lived with them.

Their son, John lived in an apartment above the house with his wife, Maxine and their eight year old daughter Audrey. John was a government employee on long term medical leave. He and I began visiting the Kenilworth Aquatic Gardens to catch turtles for a free form pond he had built in the backyard. Later we fished for yellow perch in the South River when the fish returned to fresh water to spawn.

We went to the South River from our home in Riverdale Heights via Central Avenue and on one occasion we fished the Patuxent just south of the

Queen Anne Bridge for shad. I caught one casting a Johnson Silver Minnow lure. Shad and herring no longer come up the Patuxant but the Maryland Department of Natural Resources in trying to reintroduce them.

We moved to another house when I was thirteen and I don't know about the James family after that.

When the war was nearly over and my father stopped teaching Civil Defense and Fire fighting for the University of Maryland Extension School he had more free time. Because I wanted to hunt we began to go to the woods in the Fall and early winter for that purpose. In January through March we trapped fur bearing animals such as muskrats and mink. Between the end of the trapping season to the beginning of the hunting season we fished.

Our favorite place to fish was Tridelphia Reservoir in Howard County where the Washington Suburban Sanitation Commission (WSSC) had dammed the Patuxent River. It was remote and few people were around. The water was crystal clear and only electric motors were allowed on boats. We had a 16 foot aluminum boat powered by oars. Largemouth bass were our objective but in the spring crappie congregated close to shore and you could catch all you wanted in less than an hour. One day I had hooked a crappie and was reeling him in when a huge large mouthed Bass exploded at the last moment and stole my crappie. What a thrill!

Upon graduation I worked for various electronic companies in the DC area and attended graduate school so I did not have time for fishing. Eventually I obtained a PhD in Geology/Paleontology and moved to Norfolk. Beginning at the age of 56 I taught Geology at Old Dominion University for twenty years. I retired, and when my mother was in failing health I returned to Maryland. When she passed away I recognized that I would need end of life care in the coming years. My wife, Joyce and I began visiting Continuing Care facilities,

One of those was Asbury Solomons Island in lower Calvert County. It was located on the banks of the beautiful Patuxent River. What not to like about it except that it is eighty miles to a large airport or city – too remote.

Nearby is the Calvert Marine Museum. It exceeds by far what one might expect in a small town. Located near to the end of 30 miles of cliffs along the Chesapeake Bay famous for Miocene invertebrate fossils, the area has attracted fossil collectors. Some of these collectors with deep pockets endowed the museum. As a retiring paleontologist, I wanted to give my books to a place that needed them. The Smithsonian and the U.S. Geological Survey, two entities that I worked with for some time had excellent libraries. I donated my books to the Calvert Marine Museum that sorely needed more books about Paleontology.

I have no family, nor does my wife Joyce so we wanted a place to distribute our ashes. My parents, who lived the last thirty years of their lives in Deale Beach on the Chesapeake Bay, had their ashes deposited at a favorite fishing location of my father. When my mother followed him in death a neighbor who was a charter boat captain put her ashes in the same location. The charter boat captain, George Prenant, has since died and I do not know the location. My solution is to have my ashes heaved off the Princess Anne Bridge on Central Avenue (route 214) so that they will wash into the Chesapeake. Arrangements have been made.

The Patuxent River has touched my life since I was eleven and I have touched it along most of its 110 miles. In life, the Patuxent River has intertwined with my life and will continue after I'm gone.

Fish Tales

"Down in the meadow in a little bitty pool
swam three little fishies and the mama fish, too.
Boop, boop, dit-ten, dat-tem, what-tem chu"

THE FISH THAT I caught was not in a pool but rather a pool sized body of water on the back side of the Calvert Mansion in Riverdale, Maryland. This pond was about thirty feet in diameter and had a large oak tree growing in the middle such that the open water was donut shaped and its maximum water width about ten feet. I had a light fishing rod with a spinner reel and Red and White artificial lure that was intended for large mouth bass. After just a few casts a fish attached to the lure. The fish was about a nineteen inch pickerel, a pike like fish that I had never seen. I was fourteen.

I first went fishing with my father six years earlier on a charter boat out of the Rod and Reel Restaurant in Chesapeake Beach. A group of his coworkers had organized the outing. We caught a bottom fish known as a hardhead by locals but crocker in other areas because of the sound it made. The fish were plentiful and we caught dozens weighing between two and four pounds. I fell in love with fishing. Hardhead have virtually disappeared from the Chesapeake Bay except for a few that are well under a pound.

After that time I fished the South River for migrating yellow perch with a neighbor named John James. When the war ended my father and I fished Tridelphia Reservoir in Howard County for large mouth bass and in April for crappie. This fish could be caught in the dozens when they congregated in schools near shore.

Many times I had not transportation to a fishing spot and I fished in any body of water that I could reach on foot. One of these was the pond behind the Calvert Mansion. Another time was in Paint Branch flowing through College Park. This stream separated the University of Maryland from Lakeland, a black community where university workers lived. In the 1940s Prince George's County was segregated.

I walked downstream from Route 1 until the stream speeded up around a bend. I let my lure travel downstream and then retrieved them from the rapids. On the third cast I hooked a pickerel – my second pickerel ever.

After that time I was in school and working so I had little time for fishing. That was limited to Tridelphia Reservoir where I used a light rod with four pound test nylon line.

For the next fifteen years I did not fish because of my work load. In the late 50s I took a job with Johns Hopkins University Applied Physics Laboratory in Scaggsville, Md. My job was to monitor a contract with Radiation, Inc in Melbourne, Florida for a data processing machine. That machine displayed a comparison of the Polaris flight computer caculations to the missile's actual flight path. Once when the project was not ready for a scheduled demonstration the two engineers, Ed Clagett and Buddy Mock took me fishing while the work was being completed.

Florida fishing is different from Chesapeake Bay fishing in many ways. If you fish the Bay for white perch, you only catch white perch. Fish for sea trout, sometimes called Weakfish, in Florida and you might catch bonefish, or shook or snapper or tarpon or any of the many varieties in those waters. Also, when we fished we used shrimp as bait.

Shrimp abound in the Indian River, a body of water just inland and parallel to the coastline. You could see them in schools close to shore and they could be caught easily. The shrimp we used as bait would grade 15/20, that is between fifteen and twenty per pound in a seafood store. Since I love shrimp and am so-so about fish I would have rather taken the shrimp home.

Another time we fished in Lake Hellenblazes, that portion of the St. John's River up river from Kissemee, Florida as it grades into the Everglades. You really needed a guide to fish those waters because some of the islands were floating and would move about over time. My hosts hired a guide who took us in his small boat into Lake Hellenblazes to catch large mouthed bass. This was fresh water.

The guide had a tactic when a bass took his bait. He took a cigarette out of his pocket, lit it up, and took a puff. Then he would rear back and really set the hook. He knew that the bass would take to bait ten feet or so and then turn the bait to get a better grip. We didn't boat any bass that day but caught several mudfish.

Another time when visiting Radiation, Inc. I finished my day several hours before sunset and went to the ocean shore to fish. Somewhere I had learned that there was a trough about five feet off the shoreline and fish came there to feed. That day I hooked a large fish in that trough. Somehow I saw how large it was and since I was using a very light rod with four pound test line I realized that if the fish was in the surf his weight alone would break the line. I wadded out past the breakers getting wet to my waist. I held the line for about forty-five minutes until the fish tired and I could gab hold and take him to shore. It was a nine pound channel bass sometimes called a red drum and in the New Orleans area simply a redfish. This was the biggest fish I ever caught.

This is the story of an ordinary person that loved to fish but when he had time, he had no resources and when he had resources he lacked free time. When I became a geologist and was outdoors due to field trips, I stopped fishing. I was fifty at the time. I made little dent on the fish population except one of the three little fishies is no longer in the little bitty pond.

Three Knox Road Tales

I LIVED ON Knox Road, adjacent to the University of Maryland's main campus for several years in the late 50s.The apartment was in a brick building that was divided into four units. There were about six buildings on one side of the road and nothing on the opposite side. A small creek divided the road and the road was entered from Route 1.

Most of the apartments were occupied by other students and some of these were from other countries. Some of these foreign students had friends in the DC embassies, for that reason we could always get Players cigarettes for 5 cents a pack, however few could stand to smoke these cigarettes. A Pakistani graduate student working on a Masters degree in Economics named Hamid Nez invited my wife and me for dinner with his brother Magid. He served Pakistani chicken and rice that was made with spices that I had never tasted and it was wonderful. This was my first exposure to the Pakistani or Indian food and I loved it. I make curry frequently these days remembering that delicious meal.

Another neighbor, a government employee, had a brother working for the State Department. The brother had returned from Tibet with a Tibetan temple guard dog, a Lhasa Apso. My neighbor ended up with the dog and when he realized that he couldn't keep the dog because he was not home during the day he passed it on to us. This is how I once owned one of the original Tibetan Lhasa Apsos.

There were about four hundred of these dogs brought to the US before China closed the Tibet border. We named the dog Rags. Rags weighed about 45 pounds and had a large jaw full of teeth – a formidable watchdog. He loved to lie on cold surfaces, perhaps because they were like temple floors. We named him Rags because he had long black and white hair. I witnessed him better a German Shepherd by lying on his back so the Shepherd could only bite his hair, but Rags could bite throat.

I was once offered to breed Rags by someone in New Jersey. The best I could gain was about $400, not worth a trip to New Jersey at a time when I was busy attending classes and working part time. The Llasa owners realized that the gene pool was too small to sustain a breed so they crossed them with the Maltese terrier to give us the lap dog we know today as a Lhasa Apso.

One day when I was walking Rags, I noticed in the creek that ran between the two sides of Knox Road, the telltale sign of muskrat in the form of droppings on a rock. I had trapped muskrats for two years during high school and knew how to catch them. This time I wanted to trap one for the challenge but not for pocket money. The muskrat trapping season started midnight January first. I left a New Years Eve party at twelve so the trap would be set for the maximum time before dawn. I wanted to finish up before dawn so no one would see me. I got up early that morning and sure enough I had caught a muskrat less than ten yards from my front door. Before I could pick up my trap a lady walking her dog saw me and I'm sure she wondered what I was doing walking around in hip boots at that hour.

I skinned the muskrat and stretched it out to dry as though I intended to mail it to the raw fur market but I never did send it. When my wife told a friend who lived two buildings down, the friend replied:

"Oh, thank God. When I told my husband that I had seen a very large rat in the creek that slid down the bank"

he replied,

"that is not possible, you must have had too much wine".

These three tales are very different, one is about my introduction to Indian food. Another my Lhasa Apso experience and finally the humor associated with catching a muskrat in a suburban area. Knox Road is the only connection between them.

Rocky and The Gang

JOYCE AND I were lying in bed a little after midnight one night when we heard "thunk" followed soon after by another "thunk" and the sound of something rolling across the kitchen floor. Since our intrepid watch dog, Humphrey, a basset hound, didn't move a muscle Joyce got up and went to the kitchen to check it out. We found a young raccoon, about five pounds, that had pulled a plastic liter bottle of soda from the pantry. When we turned on the light he ran out the doggie door. Rocky Raccoon seemed a good name and we hoped we had scared him, never to return.

Au Contraire! The next night we heard a noise once again and when the lights went on he left with who we assumed to be his twin. We named the twin Ricky.

We had a raccoon problem that we needed to solve. Poison, or shooting seemed dangerous in town and having a dog who spent his days in the yard. The City of Norfolk suggested that we trap the beast and offered us a Havahart trap. The best bait for the trap was an egg.

I set the trap on top of the middle bin of my compost pile about four feet off of the ground so that our dog could not reach it. It seemed to me that it would be best to break the egg. That night I caught a two pound opossum so cute I let him go.

The next night I left the egg unbroken and caught Rocky or Ricky. Fortunately my neighbor, Gene Field, offered to take the raccoon to the Great Dismal Swamp which was far enough away that the raccoon would not return. Gene was a local who managed property and had time to spare during the day. Also he was a wildlife lover who fed corn year round to the wild ducks in the water of the Lafayette River, across the street from our houses.

The next night I caught the other raccoon, thus both Ricky and Rocky, our two perps were accounted for.

I baited the trap once again and after a few nights I caught two very small baby raccoons. Oh, how pathetic they looked in that trap! We didn't name them at the time but we might have called them

Rockette and Rickette. Off to the Dismal Swamp with the two of them.

A few nights later I caught the mother of all raccoons figuratively and possibly literally. This raccoon must have weighed over twenty-five pounds and could not even turn around in the Havahart. I accompanied Gene to the Dismal Swamp where I witnessed her run off into the brush. After a while the trap was returned to the City of Norfolk, thus ending the saga.

Sausage and Me

I HAVE OFTEN joked that there are three food groups: sausage, cheese and other things. I offered this statement in jest, but in truth, sausage is my favorite food. About 20 years ago I began making my own sausage.

The best hot dogs in my estimation were the ones at Griffith Stadium watching the Washington Senators play baseball. Those dogs were simply prepared in boiling water and left in that hot water until put on a steamed roll with mustard. I always ate five or six during a ball game. Oh yeah, sometimes I also ate peanuts in the shell and Cracker Jacks.

An Alsatian dish, *choucroute garni* calls for a small diameter hot dog like Strasbourg sausage or frankfurter. When I make this dish, that I love dearly, I also include bratwurst.

My love of *choucroute garni* once led to food poisoning. At a restaurant in Nantes, France I had the dish but thought the bratwurst was undercooked. Because I trusted the French kitchen I ate it all. That night I was sick with constant diarrhea and throwing up. My wife, Joyce and I decided we would be safer at our Paris hotel because they considered us near family and would take care of us. We took a train the next day back to Paris. Our hotel in Paris belonged to a consortium that contracted for medical assistance 24/7. Even though it was a Sunday, the doctor came quickly, examined me and proclaimed–

"Monsieur, you have a microbe (he pronounced it meeecrobe)"

He gave me a shot and a prescription. By evening I was well enough for dinner but prudently opted for roast chicken, I ate it all. By the way, I no longer trust any kitchen.

My wife Joyce also likes sausage but for the first ten years of our marriage we refrained from eating commercial sausage because they contained fillers, preservatives and unknown animal parts. Then I bought a grinder with a stuffing attachment and casings, I used pork picnics as the meat because it is inexpensive and has a good flavor.

Over the next several years I made about twenty types of sausage varying from Texas wieners to Swedish sausage with potatoes. We settled on three kinds for our use: hot Italian sausage, bratwurst and spicy southern breakfast sausage.

Five years ago we moved to a senior facility that provided us with one meal a day and I put away my grinder. After about two years we tired of the repetitiveness of the meals that they prepared and began cooking again several times a week.

Two months ago I dug out my grinder, ordered new casings and started sausage making again. Oh heavenly days, I love sausage!!

A Streetcar Named
Mt. Pleasant

I GREW UP in a suburb of Washington, DC at a time when suburban shopping malls did not exist. We bought everything except groceries "downtown" – along F Street NW between 7th and 15th Streets. As a kid, I particularly liked the 5 and 10 store's pet department where I could see tropical fish such as guppies and angelfish, as well as little turtles, salamanders and white mice. Another favorite was the nut shop because the wonderful smell of roasting nuts permeated the air outside on the sidewalk. I loved cashews but they were expensive.

To get downtown we took a bus to Mt. Ranier where we caught the streetcar named Mt. Pleasant that went several miles on Rhode Island Ave. then continued crosstown along F Street and beyond. My immature mind never mused about where Mt. Pleasant was located but that area of Washington became woven into the tapestry of my life.

At age 14, I was able to get a permit to work in Washington. My first job was as a "soda jerk" at Peoples Drug Store in Georgetown. The Peoples Drug Store personnel that hired me didn't care where I lived or that it required one hour and forty-five minutes to travel from my home in Riverdale Heights to Georgetown. I was young, wanted money and just "did it". Again the bus to Mt. Ranier, the streetcar named Mt. Pleasant but in this situation I continued past F Street to 1600 Pennsylvania Ave. In front of the White House I transferred to a Rosslyn streetcar and got off on M Street just short of Wisconsin Ave. The building housing the Peoples Drug Store was very old and I found that the back stairs were deeply grooved due to many years of use. Next door was a Thom McAn shoe store where I used much of my first paycheck to buy a more comfortable pair of shoes.

In 1954, I left the Marine Corps and began attending the University of Maryland. My wife had spent some time in Mexico and spoke Spanish fluently. She found a Mexican restaurant named "El Sombrero Cordobes" which served food she had learned to love. This restaurant was on Mt. Pleasant Street in the Mt. Pleasant/Columbia Heights part of

Washington. I particularly liked the chicken soup which was made with potatoes and had a flavor that I have not found since. This taste probably resulted from some herb or spice used only in one region of Mexico.

Some people that we met in the restaurant invited us to the Saturday night dances sponsored by the Club Latinoamericano and held in the basement of the nearby Shrine of the Sacred Heart church. At this time the Latino community was only about 8000 and consisted mostly of people from the embassies and professionals such as doctors and lawyers. I'm not a very good dancer but I loved Latin music. My favorite dances were the merengue and paso doble, which I could do given sufficient lubrication.

During this time period we also visited Charlie Byrd's nightclub near Columbia Road and 18th St. Charlie was famous worldwide for his skill with the jazz and the classical (Spanish) guitar. He is given credit for introducing the Bossa Nova (think the Girl from Ipanema) to the US. Raised in Southeastern Virginia he was quoted as saying of his hometown, "a hot time on Saturday night in Chuckatuck, VA consisted of a moon pie, RC Cola, and a dirty joke". He died in Annapolis in 1999. Visiting his nightclub consisted of buying a drink and listening to a world renowned guitarist.

In 1959, Enrique Baez, a recent arrival from Castro's Cuba, opened a Cuban-Hungarian restaurant at Columbia Road and Belmont named the Omega. I assumed that Mr. Baez had had a Hungarian restaurant in Havana before he came to the US. I learned about Cuban dishes such a ropa vieja and piccadillo which were served with black beans and rice. I adore black beans and would go to the Omega not caring what the main dish was, just give me the black beans!

After that marriage failed I stopped going to the Mt. Pleasant area for awhile. The one exception was viewing the movie "War and Peace" at the Ontario Theater in 1969. To the Russians, War and Peace is a national treasure and they spared no expense in making the six and one half hour movie. I saw it with friends one Sunday. First, 3 ½ hours of movie, picnic lunch on the lawn, and then the final 3 hours of the movie. It was magnificent.

In the early 1970s I took a job in Alexandria, VA at the Seismic Data Lab. On several occasions my co-workers and I went to the Omega for lunch. By this time the Omega had grown to occupy two storefronts and had dropped Hungarian food from the menu.

In 1978, I went to Norfolk, VA to teach geology at Old Dominion University. When I returned to the DC area 22 years later the Ontario Theater was closed, the Omega no longer operated and the Shrine of the Sacred Heart was offering Mass in English, Spanish, Haitian and Vietnamese. The Latino community of Washington, DC had grown 100 fold to about 70,000 and the Mt. Pleasant/Columbia

Heights area was home to several ethnic groups, not just Latinos.

These days I sometimes go Mintwood Place, a French restaurant on Columbia Road near 18th Street where my favorite dish is porchetta, a deboned suckling pig wrapped and tied in it's own skin, cooked for a juicy interior and crisp exterior. This dish is only offered on Sundays. Last year my foot was run over by a car in front of the Mintwood on a "dark and stormy night". I was essentially unscathed.

It is astounding that a little boy's trips downtown to see the guppies and smell the roasting nuts would be linked his whole life to the destination designated on the "streetcar named Mt. Pleasant".

Marine Corps, Memphis and Things Cultural

WHERE AND WHEN do we learn things cultural that are not part of our years at home? It seems to me that life experiences are the classroom for such learning and unlikely situations for this process occurred during the three years I spent in the Marine Corps. Living in a blue collar neighborhood during the later part of the Great Depression I was previously exposed to only a narrow set of life experiences and ideas.

I joined the Marine Corp in 1951 during the Korean War and assumed that I would be sent to Korea. The Marine Corps decided otherwise based upon my very high score on the intelligence test.

They sent me to the Naval Air Technical Training Center in Millington, TN for training in maintenance and repair of aviation electronics equipment. After completing the 28 week course they assigned me to the same school in Millington as an electronics instructor for the remainder of my three year enlistment. For someone who wished to see the world, three months in Paris Island, South Carolina for basic training and 33 months in Millington, Tennessee just did not "cut it".

Memphis was a short bus ride from Millington and on weekends and each week night the bus shuttled marines and sailors back and forth to Memphis. The bus was dubbed the "vomit comet" because the return trip often carried a few drunk sailors. In Memphis there were several USOs to host the servicemen. One was "Mother's Canteen" where free donuts were always available, another the YWCA where girls were always available and a third, the JCC (Jewish Community Center) where both were available. In addition there were bars in hotels such as the Peabody and Claridge, and there was even a bar especially for Marines. But what about culture?

I had my first pizza, thin crust variety, and loved it at a little restaurant near the bus terminal. Back in DC there were no pizza parlors and pizza was only found in Italian Restaurants such as the AV Ristorante at 1st and New York Avenue. Pit barbeque gained my life long affection the first time I tried it. The only barbeque I had eaten previously was at the Hot Shoppes and was a wet, limp variety not especially appealing. One small restaurant in Memphis had pork shoulder turning invitingly in the window and tasty bean pots with hunks of pork debris heating in the same fire. I regularly enjoyed both.

When stuck on the base between paychecks, I spent my off hours reading books. I clearly remember *Lost Horizons* by James Hilton and his concept of Shangri-La. Additionally I read a number of Hemingway's novels such as *The Sun Also Rises*, *A Farewell to Arms* and *For Whom the Bell Tolls*, Mailer's *The Naked and the Dead*, Huxley's *After Many A Summer Dies the Swan* and many others.

Because there was a war on and we were servicemen, we regularly enjoyed the sounds of the big bands that performed on the base for free. I remember fondly Benny Goodman, Tommy Dorsey, Ray Anthony and Hal McIntyre. A much different sound was available in Memphis on Beale Street. One Wednesday night several of us went to the W.C. Handy Theater to hear the magnificent Lionel Hampton play his music and grunt. Although white people were not welcome at the W. C. Handy Theater on the other six days, no one that I knew objected.

Once, when I was still a student, a sailor classmate named Hugo Igoe and I decided to hitchhike to Cairo, Illinois. A large blue Cadillac stopped for us and the driver announced that he was going to St.

Louis, MO. That was Hugo's home so we bypassed Cairo in favor of St. Louis. While there we spent Saturday night in East St. Louis, IL listening to jazz. The jazz was different from any jazz that I had previously heard in that it featured abundant brass. At the end of the evening, we returned to Hugo's home, a row house similar to the row houses in much of Washington DC. We nearly froze that night because the Igoes turned off the heat at night to save money.

When I was an instructor, the instructor's lounge was also the room for the Chief Petty officers. Because most of the Navy provided instructors to the school held that rank and C.P.O. is the highest rank among enlisted men in the navy, the Chief's room was in fact a well appointed lounge. In that room I watched on television the 1953 World Series in which Billy Martin garnered a record 12 hits. Another opportunity to grow occurred because the chiefs played bridge regularly and on many occasions asked me to be the fourth player. Although in the beginning I knew nothing about bridge I soon learned what bridge was and how to play. I loved to play bridge for the fun and continued to play for many years after I was discharged from the marines. Eventually the "wonks" took over bridge insisting on formatted bidding and offering stern rebukes if mistakes were made. I stopped playing because it ceased to be fun but I remember that no-trump was my favorite suit although it was seldom bid by others.

I was introduced to a variety of tastes, sounds and intellectual activities which now seem quite ordinary. Pizza and pit barbeque, contemporary and near contemporary literature, big bands and Beale St. jazz, row houses and USOs, bridge and baseball records are parts of this "cultural" awakening. It's said that you can take a man out of his neighborhood but you can't take his neighborhood out of the man. Maybe they are just plain wrong.

Luck

I JOINED THE U.S. Marine Corps at the County Service Building in Hyattsville, was sworn in in Washington DC and traveled by train to the basic training facility on Parris Island, SC. The date was June 19, 1951. In the six months prior to joining the Marine Corps, I took a full load (19 semester hours) at the University of Maryland, played freshman tennis for the school and worked the night shift at ERCO (Engineering Research Company) in Riverdale, MD. At the time, this company was making aircraft parts for the Korean War effort but was better known for the ERCOUPE, a small plane and competition for the Piper Cub. Boot camp was good for me. With three good meals a day and enough sleep I gained 15 pounds because as rigorous as the training was, it was easy compared to my prior schedule. In addition, I learned some valuable life lessons.

Upon arriving at Parris Island, my head was shaved, I was given clothes and assigned to a platoon of 65 other recruits and two drill instructors. Then 10 weeks of basic training began with the first six weeks devoted to marching and drilling with our M-1 rifles. The drill instructors were merciless in their expectations and at the end of those six weeks we were indeed perfect.

During that July, 2 recruits died while marching in the humidity and heat of a South Carolina marsh. Restrictions were placed on the drill instructors—no outdoor marching when the temperature was above 110 degrees F. One day when we could not march outdoors, our drill instructor had us march in the barracks. The bunk beds were pushed to the center of the room and we all piled our sneakers next to the drill instructor in the middle. We marched single file around the periphery of the room and if you screwed up the drill instructor would hit you with a sneaker. The dedicated drill instructors were not about to let their platoon lack the practice necessary for perfection.

The next two weeks were spent at the rifle range. Our platoon packed its gear and marched about ten miles to temporary quarters in Quonset huts with outdoor universal toilets. Although it was called the rifle range, it in fact was a large wooded area suitable for field training and maneuvers. In the first week we learned the art of concealment, field tactics as a group, hand to hand combat and were introduced to ordnance other than our M-1s, grenades, bayonets, pistols, machine guns, carbines and browning automatic rifles.

Proficiency with the M-1 rifle is of the utmost importance to a marine. Therefore, a week was devoted to actually firing the weapon at target for a score and the final day's score determined if you qualified with the rifle. Not qualifying led to humiliation and shame. In fact you were made to wear your clothes backwards and thus everyone knew you had failed.

Each day for four days you fired 50 rounds at the bulls eye target. The fifth day was spent in the pits under the targets, lowering the target, marking the shot with a large disc and raising the target for the next shot. In this manner, the shooter and his scorer could see where the previous shot had struck the target. If in the bulls eye, the shot scored 5 points, circle around the bulls eye 4 points, then 3 to 1 points depending on closeness to the bulls eye. A perfect score was 250 points and 190 points were required to qualify.

On my second practice day, I scored especially well and I attributed that good score to the lubri-plate that I had placed in the small well in the butt of my rifle. I called it my lucky lubri-plate. Lubri-plate is a substance used to lubricate the firing mechanism.

On qualifying day I made sure that my lucky lubri-plate was in my gun butt and therefore I would not fail. The first 10 shots are taken in standing position with the target 100 yards away. The next 20 shots were from the kneeling and prone positions at a 300 yard target. Everything was on course, perhaps a little under my average. The next ten shots were taken rapid fire. That is, you fired very rapidly without benefit of knowing where the previous shot had struck. I had been a little off target and the ten rounds clustered a little to the left. I was in big trouble.

The next ten shots were to be from the prone position at a target 500 yards away. I had never gotten a score higher than 40 and I needed 42 to avoid failure. I took the lucky lubri-plate out of the gun butt and threw it as far as I could, took a deep breath and proceeded. I very carefully and patiently squeezed off each round remembering the techniques that I had learned. It worked for I scored a 45 – total 193.

I had prevailed and learned several valuable lessons from this experience. Luck is highly overrated and unlikely to be there if you need it. More importantly, that success comes from focus, hard work and inner spirit.

"Touch The Water

THERE'S AN OLD saying, "different strokes for different folks," the truth of which can be seen in the various ways that people spend their vacations. Some people want to "get away from it all" and opt for camping in the forests or near a lake where they can rough it. Others want to "get away from it all" by taking a cruise or visiting a full service resort where their every whim and need is catered to with a minimum effort on their part. A third group prefers to visit a previously not known part of the world to observe other people, cultures or societies. I fall somewhere within this third group.

For example, my wife and I have visited Paris a number of times. On the first few visits we spent an hour in the Louvre, an hour in the D'Orsay and

30 minutes in the Rodin museums, the rest of our time was spent walking around the city. The art was beautiful but the museums were all about the past. What about the present?

After those first few trips, we just walked around visiting the local markets and neighborhoods. We would take a Metro to the line's terminus and walk back through the various neighborhoods to our hotel. It was normal for us to walk between five and ten miles a day. I particularly liked the food markets in which a great variety of fruits, vegetables, seafood and meats were laid out neatly for the customers. Witnessing the customer's purchases let us know about their plans for dinner.

Each neighborhood had its own bread shop, pastry shop, butcher shop, wine store, etc. with beautiful displays of their wares in the window. Viewing these shop windows introduced us to greater varieties of food and food preparations than we normally see in the U.S. Cafes or bistros were common and we would often stop for coffee or wine to watch the people passing.

A common sight was twenty to eighty chickens in rows on a multi-rod rotisserie rotating such that the chicken juices of one row dripped upon the chickens on a lower row. These chickens looked so inviting with glistening golden brown skin and juices all over them. On several occasions we bought a chicken, a baguette (bread), cheese and wine which we took to the river bank for lunch.

On one occasion we were walking in an Algerian neighborhood in Montmartre, and my wife spotted a rotisserie in operation.

She said, "look at the beautiful chickens cooking".

I looked closely and replied "those are not chickens, they are skinned sheep heads."

My wife was mortified!

Another activity that can yield information about people and their day to day lives are road trips. For example, when I drove to Colorado to collect data and fossils for my dissertation I used Route 50 rather than the interstate. Although it took a bit more time, I saw more than Comfort Inns and Denny's.

In Kansas, Route 50 went through Russell, Kansas, home of Koch Petroleum. In the past thirty years, this company has grown and now we have the politically active "Koch brothers" – two of the richest men in the world. Further west, I went through Dodge City, home of the TV series Gunsmoke. There I saw Kitty's cafe, the Long Branch and "boot hill". Further on just before the Kansas and Colorado border was Coolidge, Kansas, a very small town consisting of several hundred residents, a co-op gas pump and a five room motel with a small cafe attached. It was in this cafe that I tasted the best chili ever and learned that the cook put both red and green chilies in the pot. These days I make my own chili this way.

Ninety miles west of Coolidge is the fairly large town of Pueblo, Colorado. Its main activity was cattle feeder lots and you could smell those lots for many miles. Here I saw the largest pile of bull poop in the world. If I had taken the interstate to Colorado, I would have missed these, and many more, interesting experiences.

I have titled this paper "touch the water" and the reader may wonder why — here's why. When I graduated from college in 1957, it freed up money my father had put away in case I had financial problems that might prevent me from finishing my education. Hard work had gotten me through and I never knew he had sequestered the money. He used the freed up money to put a new roof on the house and to buy a 16' Alumacraft boat so that he could fish the nearby Tridelphia and Rocky Gorge Reservoirs.

A few years later he built a small house in Deale Beach on the Chesapeake Bay and used his 16' boat to fish and crab. A few times each summer I would visit and take the boat into the nearby creek to crab via hand lines and chicken necks. I loved that boat because I could touch the water.

When my father obtained a permit from the state a short time later to have six offshore crab pots in the water, he religiously tended his pots daily. He discovered that sometimes when the water was rough it was too dangerous to go out in the 16' boat. He bought a larger boat.

I never liked the new boat because it rode too high and therefore I couldn't touch the water. I liked to be able to touch the water.

If there is an epiphany involved in all of this, it is that moment when I recognized that preferring the smaller boat because from it I could touch the water was not different from enjoying the markets and neighborhoods of Paris more than the museums. Road trips via the older roads rather than on the interstate highways is a similar choice. Situations involving "touch the water" decisions occur almost daily. "I like to touch the water" has become my own personal mantra.

Scars with Benefits

THE EMOTIONAL WOUNDS that we experience during our lives almost always heal and we are left with the scars. When I figuratively run my hand over my "skull" I feel the knobby bumps that remind me of the wounds. The two largest of these bumps represent two different wounds and my reactions to these were quite different. I realize that others have experienced larger and more tragic loss, for example, I have never experienced anything near the severity of losing a child. My heart goes out to those that have.

The first event was the dissolution of my marriage of thirteen years. At that time, my sole purpose was supporting my wife and daughter and when that purpose was removed I was lost. I realize now that

I did not have a life of my own. Growing up during a depression and an important war had conditioned me to believe that duty was the most important thing in life.

I was depressed for about two years. I worked but not well. Those two years were more difficult than giving up tobacco after thirty years of heavy smoking. People would say that they hoped we would get back together. An older and wiser widowed neighbor, Mr. Potter said he hoped things would work out for the best. I think that things did.

What did I want to do with my life? Although I was a successful electronics engineer, I wanted to be outdoors more and to travel. I began taking classes in Geology half time at the George Washington University while continuing to work full time as a engineer. My social life was sparse in this situation, but I met someone– Yvonne, a lovely and serious English lady who became my wife. After about a year tragedy struck and struck hard.

One morning, Yvonne got out of bed and could not stand. We visited her doctor who immediately admitted her to the Georgetown University Hospital's emergency room He correctly diagnosed that she was experiencing acute demylinization, an ailment like MS but taking place in a matter of hours, not years. Before the night was over she was unable to move any part of her body.

I visited every morning before work and every evening after work for two months. When I went to her room the TV was invariably off and I would turn it on. I had witnessed her decline and therefore I knew her mind was functioning. The nurses thought she was in a vegetative state and didn't think the TV was necessary. One time I was in her room when the nurse was giving her her pills. Reflectively she sneezed and sprayed mucous on the nurse's arm. She then grimaced and twisted into a smile. I was right, she was "in there".

After two months, I took her home. I found a high-rise in the Belle Haven area south of Alexandria that had a Physical Therapy clinic on the first floor. I hired aides to care for her and take her to PT while I worked. I manned the second and third shifts myself. Her aides cost as much as I made. When my savings were gone, Fairfax County Welfare gave me enough to survive. Part of the stipend was in food stamps and I keep one around to remind me of that fact.

After two years of doing my very best, it was apparent that she would never recover and to continue caring for her at home was futile and perhaps even foolish. I found a very nice nursing home in Manassas and took her there. During all of this tine and effort I never despaired, I was certain that this too would pass. I continued my geology courses and graduated five years later.

F. Scott Fitzgerald, the famous author of *The Great Gatsby* and *Tender is the Night* had a breakdown in his thirty's. At that time he wrote a brief essay titled *The Crack-Up* in which he talked about his illness. He felt that he had not accomplished the important things in his life. The last sentence of one paragraph towards the end was, "The old dream of being an entire man in the Goethe-Bryon-Shaw tradition, ... has been relegated to the junk heap of the shoulder pads worn for one day on the Princeton freshman football field and the overseas cap never worn overseas." He died in 1940 at the age of 44.

That passage has always resonated with me because I had joined the Marine Corps during the Korean War and expected to see combat. Because I had a vision problem the Marine Corps kept me in the United States. My dream of emulating the men of the "Greatest Generation" was relegated to my personal junk heap. The "manhood" self-image was important to me.

The tragedy of Yvonne's illness and my performance for those two difficult years left me with the feeling that I had demonstrated my inner strength. I had proven myself in a venue different than military combat. The scar comes with benefits.

Bumble Bees Can't Fly

EARLY IN 1959, I was offered a job by the Johns Hopkins University Applied Physics Laboratory (APL) in Skaggsville, MD primarily to work on a digital data acquisition system. At that time I was one of the few engineers with experience in such systems. I accepted the job and joined the Bumble Bee group. At some time in the past scientists in this group had proven that the bumble bee can't fly earning the group the name and the name stuck. Special Projects of the Navy Department had given APL the mission of evaluating the Polaris Missile's guidance system.

The Polaris Missile and its later versions, the Poseidon and Trident were the most important systems for the defense of the US because they were on board submarines and could avoid detection by hiding underwater. The Polaris guidance system was the first to utilize a digital computer and the first to use digital telemetry of its status. Can you imagine a world without digital equipment?? Think slide rules.

My task was to assure the successful construction and operation of a digital data acquisition system for the guidance system evaluations. The system was designed to display the actual missile recorded path alongside the predicted path so that the guidance programs could be adjusted. I read the contractor's proposal that served as the basis of the contract for the equipment and discovered that the system would not work as proposed. I immediately called the vendor, Radiation Inc. in Melbourne, Fl and spoke to Buddy Mock, one of the engineers on the job. When I told him of my concerns, he replied "Mr. Koch, we are not new at this game but thanks for your concern". The next day I received a frantic phone call to the effect that I was correct in my calculations and offering a solution. Had this problem not been detected until the equipment tests the equipment would not have been ready when needed.

Subsequently I became very close friends with Buddy Mock and the other engineer, Ed Claggett. Whenever I visited Florida, the three of us would fish together. Sebastian Inlet, the Indian River, the surf off Indiatlantic Beach and Lake Hell and Blazes just south of Kissimmee on the St. Johns River were four of the fishing venues. Each was a totally different type of fishing, catching different species of fish, using different baits and tackle in different water energy regimes. Back home in Maryland, the fish and the bait are mostly determined by the time of the year. Truthfully, I would prefer to eat the large shrimp that we used to catch sea trout in the Indian River, to any of the fish that were caught either place.

The computer programmers at APL were skilled at spread sheets and scientific calculations but had never worked on formatting data for a plot. After a few meetings and much give and take, these programmers recognized what had to be done and did it. The project was a huge success and on time as was the Polaris Missile. APL personnel that worked on the Polaris Missile guidance were awarded a "Certificate of Merit" for outstanding service to the Department of the Navy in the field of ballistic missile systems development and analysis etc, in December, 1960. I cherish my certificate because the Polaris Missile proved to be so important to the U.S. national defense during the Cold War with Russia and I had played a small role.

Caring Co-Workers

MY TWENTY-SIX YEAR career in electronics came to an end when I accepted a contract to teach geology courses at Old Dominion University (ODU) for the spring semester, 1978. Those twenty-six years were jammed full of life experiences, fulfilling employment and academic achievement. I will always remember and appreciate those that helped me during those years, especially my co-workers whose motivation may have been just helping another to get ahead.

I joined the Marine Corps during the Korean War hoping to see the world. Unfortunately the Marine Corps decided I was not "canon fodder" material and sent me to a Navy aviation electronics school in Millington, TN. Looking back I would change the unfortunately to fortunately because I am still alive. I was then assigned to remain in Millington as an electronics instructor. With a wife and very young daughter, I left the Marine Corps determined to study electronics engineering at a good university.

To support this family after my discharge, I needed to supplement my GI bill stipend with part-time employment that would allow me to attend college. Businesses do not often employ entry level people part-time but I got lucky. The next door neighbor of my parents, Jack Salmon, worked at the Naval Ordnance Lab (NOL) in White Oak, MD and he helped me get a position there as a student trainee (WAE), paid "when actually employed". This allowed me to work part-time with a schedule that could accommodate my classes at the nearby University of Maryland. I worked as much as I could, sometimes to the detriment of my classes.

The unit that I worked in was titled Environmental Testing Division. This was 1954, more than eight years before Rachel Carson published her iconic book about danger to the environment, *Silent Spring.* The environmental testing had nothing to do with the general environment and everything to do with the environment experienced by naval ordnance. My job was not very exotic— dropping ball switches from various heights to measure the energy/impact necessary to successfully operate the switch.

For two years, I commuted between my home, the University of Maryland, and the NOL. Usually

I could work between 30-35 hours a week. I never missed a day and I never "goofed off". Because of my Marine training, I had experience with radar and advanced instruments such as the cathode-ray oscilloscopes. When my group purchased these devices for ordnance testing, I seemed to be the one capable of making them work. Being the youngest and having such skills may have made me a very early "techno-nerd" similar to today's teenagers that can do it all with computers and cell phones.

With a tight schedule, I sometimes put off the more mundane tasks of my classes. At the end of the first semester I needed to produce ten mechanical drawings that I had put off during the semester for the Drafting class. When my co-workers heard that I planned a two day drafting marathon at home, they offered to help. The boss, George Stamoupolous, left the office for parts unknown, Bob Chadwich, a mechanical engineer from Wooster, Mass., laid out the various prospectives and Jaime Cousins, our draftsman, made the drawings and I lettered the work. In two hours we had finished and I will always appreciate that these three men helped in this way.

The next semester, I delayed my electrical engineering lab reports until the end. Fortunately for me, the newest member of our group, Luigi Vagnoni, was a recent electrical engineering graduate from the University of Maryland and had taken the same lab course. He dug out his two year old lab reports and gave them to me. I copied his lab results, graphs and data, turned in my reports on time and passes the course. I felt no guilt, since I had had ample lab experience in the Marines. As the Beatles song goes, I got "by with a little help from my friends".

After graduation, I immediately became involved with digital systems, the newest development in electronics. Minneapolis Honeywell had me oversee the construction of a digital data acquisition system that they had purchased the rights to from Rocketdyne in California. It was the first system of this kind.

Double Gourmet

THIS IS THE story of a love born thirty years ago that has grown in depth and breadth every day since. Some time couples play the silly game of "I love you more than a bushel or I love you a million-trillion times more." I put that to rest by claiming that "the word has not been created to describe the magnitude of my love for you."

I was standing on the wooden deck adjacent to the dining area of a fine cuisine restaurant in Great Bridge, VA, south of Norfolk. Over the rail was water of the George Washington Canal. With me were about twenty other people assembled for a meal hosted by Singles Gourmet. Singles Gourmet is a wonderful club for mature singles who love to eat out at fine restaurants but not alone!

The members paid about fifty dollars to join and each meal a little extra to cover the hostess's expenses. At dinner you sat at a round table with 4 or 5 others for conversation and a lovely meal. Since no one was on a one-on-one date you could relax and enjoy.

During cocktail time before the meal, I talked to several people at length. One tall, trim brunette caught my interest. Her name was Joyce. At the next dinner she attended and I talked to her almost exclusively. Soon after that we had a dinner date for just the two of us.

As the relationship grew we saw each other more often. We went away for a weekend at a bed and breakfast in Ashburn, a town about one hundred miles north of Norfolk. On the road between the small town of Thornberg and Ashburn we saw a bluebird. This soon began being called our "bluebird of happiness." We saw no other bluebirds until we arrived at Collington where bluebirds are often seen.

We spent most of this weekend talking about our lives, dreams and expectations. Towards the end of the weekend I blurted out "Well, I guess we should get married!" I had been married before but for Joyce it was to be her first marriage. We married about six months later. Our wedding was held at the home of a friend which overlooked the Lafayette River, a gorgeous venue. The marriage was performed by the Norfolk marriage commissioner, Rufus Tonelson.

I was a tenured full professor in the Geology Department of Old Dominion University and Joyce was the Head Nurse of Labor and Delivery at DePaul Hospital. My schedule was dependent on which classes I taught that semester and Joyce usually finished her day at 3:00 pm. When Joyce got home we talked over a glass of wine about our days and other matters – that we had ample time to talk may account for the smoothness of our relationship.

We were later joined by a five or six year old French Bassett hound that we named Humphrey. Humphrey had wandered into our yard one day and probably because I fed him stayed until I returned from work. Joyce advertized for the owner but after one day began to pray that no one would answer. No one did, so Humphrey became part of our family and yes, he slept with us on a bed that I specifically built to accommodate the three of us!

I retired in 1993 but Joyce continued to work part time. After my father died my mother was alone and needed 24/7 care. We moved to Annapolis in early 2000 just after a wonderful seven course millennial meal at our home. Just before we moved Humphrey died and therefore moving was not a trauma for him.

In Annapolis we rented a house for a year and then bought a house across the street! It had a fenced in yard and a doggie door in the basement which was frequented by our newly purchased beagle puppy named Sophie. Joyce took a part time job in a fertility clinic while Sophie and I built a raised bed garden and took walks around the neighborhood. Joyce came home around three and we continued our habit of talking about our day.

Joyce's mother lived in a Continuing Care facility on Signal Mountain near Chattanooga, TN. We knew that someday we should be in such a facility. At the right time we looked for a CCRC and found Collington. We believe it was a wise choice. We love it here.

This love story was made easy because wherever we were we had a time each day to talk about everything. I believe that our love has grown because talking led to understanding and understanding each other has made our love grow stronger each day. Oh! How sweet it is!

Compelled to Garden

GROWING UP DURING the Great Depression my parents, who struggled daily to put food on the table, often impressed my siblings and me with the importance of not wasting any thing. To this day that imprinting at an early age has stuck with me. Being compelled to avoid waste led indirectly to me becoming a gardener.

My first house was about thirty years old in a nice neighborhood of Norfolk, VA – Larchmont. The oak tree in front had grown to a very large size and produced abundant leaves in the fall. The first years I stuffed these leaves into seven large black plastic bags and put them out to go to the landfill. These were my leaves, from my oak tree and I had wasted them. My God!

For several months I had been watching "Crockett's Victory Garden" on Saturday mornings, a time of relaxation from an intense week of teaching, publishing and the committee work typical of a college professor. We had a victory garden during World War Two when I was in my early teens and I always planted two or three tomato plants wherever I lived because I loved fresh vine ripened tomatoes. My interest in gardening was minimal but when Crockett showed the viewers how to build a three bin compost pile I saw a use for all those leaves – I would compost them.

Crockett's composter was made of two X fours and hog wire. Standing thirty-two inches high with three three X three bins it was easy to build. I modified his design to make the first bin four X three because two X fours came in ten foot length and I thought "why throw away that extra foot" besides the first bin needed to hold more volume.

I filled the first bin with dry leaves and some fresh grass clippings that fall. After several months, I turned the first bin's contents into the second. That spring I turned the pile once again into the third (storage) bin. At that time I had great compost or "black gold" as it is referred to by gardeners. I could not waste such a valuable material.

Very little of my yard had more than four hours of sunlight each day so to make the most of those areas I built raised beds. I grew all sorts of herbs and vegetables – tomatoes, and large green New Mexico chiles for green chile stew and chilies rellanos were my pride and joy. My need to not waste had compelled me to garden.

Shitake mushrooms were the most unusual crop that I have ever grown. Shitakies don't use soil, compost or sunlight. They are grown on oak logs. A colleague at the university in the biology department, Bryan, wanted to grow shitake but had no yard, I wanted to grow shitakies but didn't have the knowledge. So I obtained the oak logs and Bryan grew shitake spore on short pieces of dowel in his laboratory. We drilled the logs, tapped the impregnated dowels into the logs and waited. It was a lovely sight to see the mushrooms growing on the logs. Shitake mushrooms are delicious.

We moved to the Hillsmere section of Annapolis after twenty years of gardening in Norfolk. Later we rode by our former home in Norfolk and saw that the new owners had cut all the bushes in the front and took down the compost bins, and removed the raised bed frames. They had no interest in gardens and feared the compost bins would attract vermin.

The house in Annapolis was over forty years old but had a much larger yard. I did a "sun survey" at first by noting the sunny parts of the yard each hour each Saturday. No parts had more than five hours a day which meant I could grow stuff but not as fast as possible in an open field.

The best location had been used as a dog run with an anchor fence all around. The dog had been a digger so the periphery was lined with buried cement blocks and poured concrete. Removing these materials was difficult manual labor and this effort cleared the dirt along the fence for raised beds. I was very fit when I finished. The raised beds were made of 2X12 boards buried several inches into the soil. The fence served to tie up tomatoes and peppers. It also kept our cute little beagle, Sophie, from playing in my garden!

My compost bins were in the shade at the back of the fenced area. I planted a dozen tomato plants, New Mexico green chiles for chile rellanos, Chili de Arbol, a small red chile that I used for cooking, kale, lettuce and herbs. As I aged I replaced most of the annuals with the perennial black and red raspberries assuring that I need not spade or turn over many of the beds.

When I no longer could garden Joyce and I moved to a continuing care retirement community (CCRC). I had a few tomato plants for the first three years but then gave that up. Now my major time consuming activities are cooking and writing. I am glad that I was compelled by need to avoid waste to garden. It resulted in thirty years of very rewarding outside activity that kept me fit in a natural way.

Cooking Happy

THE "ACTIVITY OF cooking" captured my attention and passion late in my sixth decade. I embraced this activity as a major part of daily interest and routine for the subsequent 25 years, only stopping when I moved into continuing care facilities that provided one meal a day as part of the fee. What is the difference between cooking and the "activity of cooking"? is a question that I can only answer with the vague suggestion that cooking is preparing food for dinner and the "activity of cooking" are the various tasks that one does to prepare a meal. You might like cooking but abhor all the chopping, cutting, grinding, mixing etc. that is required. Short cuts, prepared food, canned or frozen, food processors are fair game in cooking but never used when you love the "activity of cooking".

Prior to this epiphany, my food preparation experience was limited to dressing chickens or fish for the kitchen, shucking oysters, grilling hot dogs, hamburgers and chickens, pit roasting hundred pound pigs and making a cup of instant coffee. I eased into the "activity of cooking" very unplanned and innocently. After my wife Joyce and I married, she prepared our dinners. One of her favorite ingredients was boneless, skinless chicken breast. Since these chicken parts were expensive relative to whole chickens, I calculated that I could buy a chicken and cut out the breasts for the same cost. The rest of the carcass was essentially free and I stored these in the freezer. The freezer became full so from time to time I would make chicken soup with the carcasses. I enjoyed chopping the vegetables and cutting up the chickens, The soup was delicious. This was the beginning of the "activity of cooking". The freezer full of chicken carcasses reminds me of a sign I once saw while on a field trip to Texas south of San Antonio. My colleague and I stopped for gas in Uvalde, Texas and on the door was a sign reading: The armadillo buyer will be at Minimart No. 6 between 2:00 pm and 2:15 pm on Saturday, May 4th. It instructed that the armadillo be shot in the head and frozen. I have mused that some Texas boy had collected some armadillos, put them in his mother's freezer, but missed the buyer. Back into the freezer with the animals, sorry mom!

I made chicken soup with rice, with noodles, sometimes with mushrooms. A colleague of mine from the biology department and I combined our talents and raised the very tasty shitake mushrooms. They were excellent in the soup. Once I found a large edible mushroom called a puff ball and I put the whole thing in a batch of chicken soup. It made me ill.

From chicken soup, I progressed to dishes that I like but were not available prepared my way. Black beans were only offered in a small Cuban restaurant on Columbia Road in northwest Washington, DC. A coworker at the seismic lab where I worked was married to a Peruvian woman. He obtained his mother-in-law's recipe. Whenever I took black beans to a party or pot luck supper they were a big hit. This was in the days when dry black beans were not available in most grocery stores. I moved on to oyster stew using my mother's recipe and crab cakes like those of the iconic Faidley's in Lexington Market of Baltimore. My lunch hours were sometimes spent in used book stores buying cookbooks for a variety of cuisines. French regional cooking, Spanish dishes, a New York butcher's favorite recipes, crock pot cooking, seafood recipes, Creole dishes, hot and spicy, Danube region, southwest France (think fois gras and cassoulet) and others. Also available at that time were TV cooking shows which showed techniques along with dishes. Particularly helpful were Madeleine Kammen and Pierre Franey. I ingested this information and began cooking all of our meals everyday. I loved the activity and each day went to the kitchen into that special world that made me happy. I was fearless. I could successfully cook anything that I liked to eat, whether it was a simple sauteing of a rockfish filet on top of the stove or a cassoulet which starts with a couple of ducks and takes several weeks. The ducks were "confited", three different sausages made from scratch, cooking in a "baine marie" and on and on. I loved to make cassoulet, paella, chicken and shrimp gumbo, picadillo, rigatoni Nicoise, and curry – the more time consuming the better (read that as the more cooking activity the better).

Over the years my knowledge increased and my techniques improved to the point that I owned the kitchen. Even now, when I no longer cook every day I feel competent in the kitchen. If Joyce wants a cheese omelet, I just do a little ballet and out comes a perfect omelet. It should be obvious to the reader that I found happiness in the kitchen, not for just a day, but for 25 years. By following my instincts, a whole new me emerged. Try it—it might work for you also.

A Few Wonderful Days in Western Kansas

THE WESTERN INTERIOR of North America was covered by a vast inland sea several times before 65 million years ago. One such inland sea existed in Upper Cretaceous times – about 90 million years ago and I chose to study the mollusk of this sea for my dissertation. In the fall of 1976 I traveled by car from Washington, DC to localities in the west to collect fossil specimens and to peruse existing collections housed at the U.S. Geological Survey facility in Golden, Colorado.

The first stop was Russell, Kansas, a town in the center of the state made famous as the birthplace of Bob Dole. At that time the largest business in Russell was an oil drilling business owned by the Koch brothers. Today, the Koch brothers are noteworthy as billionaire contributors to right wing causes and are often in the news. I dined at the local Ramada Inn that first night and people were curious about me because my surname is also Koch.

In the morning I traveled east of Russell to Buffalo Gap, a location known to have rocks deposited 90 million years ago. The outcrop was a road cut about 40 feet high composed of thin limestone layers, I found the rocks that I wanted to collect about 20 feet up and proceeded to fill collecting bags with material. Suddenly some debris from above came down and I looked up to see a panicked coyote scrambling back to the top. The animal apparently became curious at the noise I made and leaned over too far. This was a treat since I love to see wildlife of all kinds and we did not have coyotes in Maryland 40 years ago.

The next day I traveled to Coolidge, Kansas, a small town on Route 50 a few miles from the Kansas/Colorado boundary. At that time the town consisted of a grain elevator, a co-op gas pump and a 5 room motel with a small cafe attached. The population of Coolidge was less that 100 people. This is high prairie country where cattle are grazed at about one head per acre and most people lived on ranches of may hundreds of acres.

A few miles east of Coolidge, I stopped to talk to a rancher along a fence line. I asked him about Bridge

Creek, the location that I wished to collect and he said it was on his property. I made a quick tour of the situation so that I would be prepared the next morning. After about an hour there I proceeded to the motel in Coolidge for the night. When I checked in, the manager knew everything about my origin and purpose.

Evidently the rancher wasted no time getting to the little cafe and telling his buddies all about me.

That night I had my evening meal in the little cafe – a big bowl of chili. It was delicious, in fact, it was the best chili I had ever eaten. I asked about the chili and was told that he put some green chiles in with the red chiles. I have since learned that most award winning chili includes some green chiles and I always make my chili with both types.

The next morning I returned to the ranch and began to investigate the dry creek bed of Bridge Creek. When I found the limestone of the proper age I began to break off pieces to collect using a hammer. After about one hour, I looked up to see a pronghorn antelope buck with his harem of eight checking me out. Evidently life is boring on the high prairie even for the antelope.

For my trip to the Western Interior, my days in Kansas were the most interesting, When I think about the Koch brothers and coyote in Russell, or the chili and antelopes in Coolidge it makes me smile. Few have the pleasure of relating to such a sparsely populated but beautiful place.

Tests and Prior Knowledge

S EVERAL TIMES I have taken tests about class material for which I had prior knowledge. On one occasion this helped me and another time it worked to my disadvantage.

For my PhD in Geology at the George Washington University I selected the research tools of Spanish and computers. For me learning a computer language (FORTRAN) was easy, but a foreign language – not so much. Format of the Spanish course was; attend class, read some new material, be tested on that new material. If you passed that in-class test you had completed the course. For one class the new material was about Cuban history and I already knew some Cuban history. I've always been a history buff and just happened to have read about Cuba.

I was waiting to start the next class when the instructor came by. She asked why I was there because I had passed the test last class. This was a time in my life when I was very stressed and not having to attend further classes was a tremendous relief.

I've always been a slow reader and studying electrical engineering only decreased my reading speed. The company where I worked also noted that engineers are slow readers and believed that their technical personnel would produce more if they could read faster.

That company was MEMCO in College Park and they selected a speed reading consultant for that purpose, but first they had to test for reading speed. This was in order to divide slow readers from those that were fast readers.

For the test we all watched on a screen that showed a line of text. The speed at which the text was changed increased with time until it virtually flashed momentarily on the screen. Then we took a comprehension test.

The subject of the text was the life habits of crows. As an outdoorsman I had been hunting, fishing and trapping for many years. I already knew about crows. I aced the test and was judged to be a fast reader. They assigned me to the fast reader group in which I was lost among the fast readers. I never improved my speed. Prior knowledge worked to my disadvantage.

Humorous
Mid-Management
Meetings

I N THE EARLY 1970s I was the computer services manager for the Seismic Data Laboratory in Alexandria, VA, and therefore periodically attended meetings with the other managers. These meetings discussed budgets, personnel, marketing facilities, etc. all subjects not likely to entertain the participant.

On two occasions however, discussions were humorous and/or interesting. The Seismic Data Lab's parent company was Geotech, an oil industry instrument manufacturer in Garland, TX with a reputation of treating their employees as family.

They paid low salaries but gave the employees gifts from time to time. At one meeting the CEO, Dr. Van announced that in order to save money, the company would give each employee a Thanksgiving turkey instead of the usual ham. He said "this will save the company $6000". To this I immediately replied "why not give each employee a packet of chitlins and save even more money"? Laughs all around including Dr. Van.

On another occasion Dr. Van announced that the high power computer consultant we used (Dennis Johnson) had agreed to join us as a full time employee with one stipulation – that he join us as Carol Johnson. He was just starting a sex change regimen.

The questions were: Did we think the staff would object to such an individual and what bathroom would that individual use? In the end, the staff did not object and one bathroom was marked "Please lock when in use". Forty seven years later, North Carolina, Texas and a few other states seem incapable of dealing with the transgender problem.

Her Name was
Nancy Bradley

NANCY BRADLEY WAS my instructor for a non-credit, off-campus, community accessible class in Conversational French. I had a grant to study fossils in Western Europe and because most of the seventeen weeks would be spent in Paris and Toulouse, I wanted some ability to speak French.

Nancy Bradley was a tall, straight, sixty something woman who always looked as if she just came from a tea with cucumber sandwiches. You would guess she had attended one of the seven sister colleges. She lived alone in a large frame house on a Magnolia lined street just off the Old Dominion

University campus. Sometimes she allowed a foreign student to live there in exchange for doing chores. She was a truly nice person.

The 8-10 person class would meet at her house once a week. We had a text book and workbook to use at home. She also introduced the class to French culture by talking about Champagne and cheese. We once shared a bottle of Moët Chandon and another time tasted chevre, the goat cheese. I teased her by claiming that chevre tasted like chalk.

Only two students were ever prepared for the class, myself and Judi (Jeudi in French). The others included a lawyer and a businessman. After about six weeks Nancy Bradley said we would speak only French in the next class. You guessed it! No one but Judi and I came prepared. For the rest, the class had little importance. I took the course three times and each time the same thing happened.

Nancy Bradley's hope for students to learn to speak French did not happen. Of course I was disappointed that I never got to try. The instructor's disappointment exceeded mine by a very large factor. This raises the question: do people that take a class of this sort have an obligation to their classmates and instructor?

Nancy Bradley and I had become friends. When she learned that I would be in Paris at the same time as she, she invited my wife, Joyce, and me for a glass of wine and hors d'oeuvres at the 12th floor apartment of her close friend. This apartment had a view of Notre Dame Cathedral, the Louvre and much of Paris.

Why Nancy Bradley had invited us is unknown. Perhaps it was my sense of humor or my willingness to work in class. It could have something to do with the fact that I was a full professor which is a big deal at the University. In any case I was flattered and delighted.

When Joyce and I arrived at the apartment, Nancy Bradley's friend was not home yet. Nancy gave us a glass of wine and some light hors d'oeuvres. When her friend arrived she looked at the table and stated "you don't serve that kind of food to a man!" She then opened a can of fois gras for me. I love fois gras.

Nancy Bradley was a wonderful person and I will never forget the times in class and in Paris that I spent with her.

Mrs. Macgill and Her Little Sister

MRS. MACGILL WAS a Howard County, MD farm woman with whom my first wife, Julie shared a semi-private room in the 12 bed Laurel Hospital in 1960. How Julie came to be a patient of Dr. John Warren, the hospital's founder I do not remember. We lived in College Park. I was a part time graduate student in Electrical Engineering and a full time engineer at the Johns Hopkins University's Applied Physics Laboratory working on the Polaris missile systems test and evaluation.

After a few days together in the hospital room, Mrs. Macgill invited Julie and me to her home for dinner and to play bridge with her and her little sister.

We accepted because Mrs. Macgill was in her 80s and probably a bit lonely living on a large farm. We drove to Howard County one evening in early April, up route 29, down a tree-lined, straight, one mile driveway to find a stately Federal Period mansion. In the foyer was a bottle of Southern Comfort and glasses on a small table. Much of the mansion was sealed off to save heat and we had a drink in the dining room.

It was there that we met her little sister, age 81. Her name was Edith Clark and her history was astonishing. She had attended Vassar, taken sociology and gone to China to "save the masses". After a short time she concluded that the masses were not worth saving. She earned a PhD at MIT and took a job with G.E. She advanced in the company until she became assistant to the famous inventor, Tesla. Next came a faculty appointment at the University of Texas as an Electrical Engineering professor. She wrote a text book for Electrical Engineering that was used throughout the United States. WOW! What a grand and accomplished person to meet in the middle of rural Howard County, or any place else.

After dinner we played bridge. At that time bridge was played for fun, not bound, as it is today by so many rules, conventions or so much frowning. Julie and I won but I have never been convinced that the sisters did not throw the game because they so enjoyed the company of younger people. In all, this evening was one of the most memorable of my life.

In 2014, my wife Joyce and I visited that house. We had learned through the Collington's Weekly Courier that it was now a restaurant named the King's Contrivance and had been there for many years. On a beautiful spring day we went for lunch. You no longer enter from route 29 but the grounds were still beautiful with flowers and flowering trees in full bloom. We entered in the foyer that I remembered with a table, but no bottle of Southern Comfort. The room where I dined 54 years ago was now the bar. We ate on the porch that was closed previously to preserve heat. A great meal in a grand house that evoked fabulous memories of a past time.

More Than Chicken Kiev

IMAGINE A PIPING hot, golden brown breaded, boneless skinless chicken breast on your plate and when you cut it, warm tarragon infused butter spurts out. This is a description of chicken Kiev the first time I ordered it. The taste and aroma were divine

Nearly fifty years ago a small group of conferees drove way out Geary Street from the San Francisco convention center to the Russian Renaissance restaurant in Little Russia for dinner. Because I was not familiar with the cuisine, the only dish on the menu that seemed safe was chicken Kiev. I didn't know what to expect, I had never even seen the dish. My dinner, as described in the first paragraph was beautiful, tasty, and the aroma was sensational. I vowed to have chicken Kiev again.

A few years later, on a business trip to New York I visited the famous Russian Tea Room which is located across the street from Central Park. The Chicken Kiev was a disappointment – limp, pale and virtually tasteless. The restaurant was huge with maybe eighty tables. Its kitchen must have produced chicken Kiev on an assembly line but this is a dish that needs to be served immediately after being prepared.

In 1990 I accompanied my wife Joyce to visit her friend Ann in San Francisco. To my bad luck, the Russian Renaissance was closed for renovations but it reopened and is now in its sixtieth year. A group went to another Russian restaurant but the chicken Kiev was not as good.

Joyce and I have always loved to visit Paris however, as we have gotten older the transatlantic flight became a dreaded chore. To avoid the long flight we went to Montreal instead. We called it Paris-lite because of its French culture –and it was much closer. The two times we went to Montreal, we stayed within a few blocks of the museum district, an area we enjoyed walking around. Our favorite restaurants were close to our hotel, the L'Entrecote for steak frites, the Orchide for Chinese food and Cora's for a breakfast fit for a laborer.

We had chicken Kiev at two Russian restaurants in the museum district, the Russe Kalinka and the

Troika but neither made the dish as good as the Russian Renaissance. One restaurant, the Troika, was expensive and large but the second was just one store front wide. It was at this place that we witnessed an interesting set of events.

This small restaurant had been rearranged for a party. Only two tables for two persons were set in the front area. Several long tables occupied the remaining space. At those tables were two wedding parties which seemed to be made up of an Hispanic man with some of his family and a taller, beautiful young Russian woman. In the back was a Russian trio comprised of an accordion, guitar and balalaika playing music.

As the evening went on and much vodka was consumed, several more musicians arrived and dancing commenced. One of the Russian brides was very outgoing and danced on the table. The other was quieter but was obviously enjoying herself. We were sure everyone was having a happy time.

It occurred to Joyce and me that this restaurant had a second business, or perhaps serving food was the second business and its main focus was arranging marriages between Canadian men and Russian girls. Midway through the evening another couple sat at the other table for two. They seemed to be meeting for the first time. We went for chicken Kiev but witnessed an evening of gaiety, marriage celebration and perhaps intrigue.

Many years have passed since my wonderful experience at the Russian Renaissance. Perhaps, like many things in my life, such as the first taste of vintage wine, first kiss, eating fois gras for the first time etc., subsequent experiences never are as good. My first chicken Kiev seems destined to be the best.

London Honeymoon Deluxe

JOYCE AND I went on our honeymoon to London about three weeks after our wedding. We knew that during the days between Christmas and New Years the city is virtually abandoned because office workers stay home, country people stay in their villages and tourists do not routinely visit.

Our flight to London necessitated a stop at Paris' Orly airport and we took a much smaller plane on to Gatwick Airport. Because we had flown all night we were given the best seats and champagne. Very deluxe.

My colleague, Jake Hancock, an Imperial College professor booked us a room in the Kensington area of London. We took a cab to our hotel and found the room was a major disappointment. It was located in the far reaches of the building and the room was trapezoidal. You could not get from one side of the bed to the other without climbing over the bed. It seems that a large group of French students had booked rooms and they wanted to keep the group together. Also, the management thought that we would not like noisy neighbors.

That afternoon we walked around the Kensington area looking at several museums and of course Harrods, the iconic London Department store. By the way, did you hear about the woman that bought a can of sardines at Harrods and after it was wrapped she started to leave. The clerk stopped her and said he would take it to her car. When she hesitated and looked puzzled, he said: "please, Madame should schlep"?

The next morning we woke up rested and determined to find a better room in another hotel. Joyce had learned, perhaps from a guide book, about the Rubens Hotel across the road from Buckingham Palace. After a quick call to see if they had a vacancy we took a taxi to the Rubens. At the hotel we learned that the least expensive room was 400£ (about $600). There we were in the lobby of the Rubens with our luggage, faced with a room price we could not afford.

The reception clerk noticed our chagrin and said:

"at Victoria Station there is a hotel rental office for people coming off of the trains and that sometimes when a hotel is under booked it will offer its rooms at a heavily discounted price. The Rubens had done just that and we should walk the five blocks to Victoria Station and book through them. He added that we could leave our luggage in the Rubens lobby and that he would watch it"

We walked to Victoria Station and booked a room at the Rubens. The price was still more than we had planned to spend but it was our honeymoon and we had been "floating" for two days. We were very happy. We may have mentioned in our conversations with the reception clerk that we were on our honeymoon because he gave us a suite (bedroom, sitting room, large bath on the fifth floor). Further, we learned that no one else was staying on the fifth. In the morning although we had paid for a continental breakfast we were told there was no continental breakfast that week. We were "forced" to eat the full breakfast buffet. The buffet had everything, six kinds of eggs, six types of meats, hot and cold cereals, breads, rolls, biscuits "mushers", baked beans, pastries, and many beverages. The deluxe accommodations and breakfast was suitable for the wealthiest honeymooners.

The next day we set out to see the sights of London. First stop was across the street at Buckingham Palace where we witnessed the "changing of the guard". The guards were not the fancy ceremonial guard but the actual real Palace guards. They are the Gurkha troops noted for their bravery and fierce fighting spirit. These small, dark men in khaki uniforms are from Nepal and their motto is "better to die than be a coward".

Next we took the "tube" to Leicester Square and walked up Charring Cross Road. *84 Charring Cross Road* is the title of a well known novel set in a bookstore at that address but we found a record store now occupied the spot.

Across Charring Cross Road at about that point is Old Compton Street, the entrance to London's racy Soho District. Just a half block in we found an Indian restaurant named Passage to India and we have eaten there many times on subsequent trips. There are many other nice restaurants in Soho, especially along Old Compton Street. In the heart of Soho was Paul Raymond's Revue bar that was somewhat famous at that time and featured very pretty women, often nude. It was the first to show full frontal nudity in Great Britain and the life of Paul Raymond was made into a movie in 1989. The show bar closed in 2004 and is now a gay bar.

The following day we visited Covent Garden and its nearby markets. I always visit markets because they show the produce, seafood and meats that the locals eat. Also, I'm a devout "foodie". We walked to the British Museum and spent most of the time there viewing ancient Egyptian, Greek and Roman sculptures. The Rosetta Stone was much smaller than I expected.

The next several days were similar. We took the tube to one of the well known sites, walked around and returned to the Rubens for a nap. At dinner we didn't want to get back on the tube because we were tired but rather walked to Victoria Street in front of Victoria Station. Along that street were dozens of restaurants to accommodate the visitors and these restaurants were virtually empty. We could get a good meal of any ethnic type we wished quickly and at a reasonable price.

Each time we walked to Victoria Street we passed a Barkley's Bank and I was reminded that the Barkley Currency Exchange at Gatwick Airport had cheated us. When I converted some French Franks to English pounds the cashier had punched up the exchange rate for Belgium Francs and I was shorted about nine dollars. I didn't notice until I had stepped away from the window. This bugged me, so one day we stopped in the Barkley Bank and talked to a Vice President. I told him that I didn't want the money but wanted him to know that he might have a "bad seed" at Gatwick. He was courteous, thanked me and while we talked he had a check cut for nine dollars. I was no longer bugged.

On New Years Eve we went to Trafalgar Square, London's equivalent to New York's Time Square. The people were so thick that we left because Joyce becomes somewhat claustrophobic in large crowds.

New Years Day we checked out Piccadilly Circus and to our good fortune witnessed the first ever

Mayor of Westminster's New Years Day Parade. It consisted of only a few cars and maybe one band. It was meager and held on the coldest day of our visit.

That was thirty years ago and things have changed. Now, the New Years Day Parade is huge and many American high school bands raise cash all year in order to participate. The city is no longer empty between Christmas and New Years but full of southern Europeans taking advantage of cheap air fares. The hotel reservation business at Victoria Station is gone because the hotels are always full.

This honeymoon trip turned out to be the experience of a lifetime. Neither of us had a history of frivolous spending because of our upbringing. I was a child during the depression and Joyce was raised by a single mom until she was twelve. This "imprint" stays with you the rest of your life.

We went on this London honeymoon expecting to get the trip we could afford. We got so much more, a honeymoon suite, wonderful breakfasts and free drinks on the shuttle from Paris. We had a champagne honeymoon on a beer budget.

Wine Thoughts

I N MARCH 2015 I received an e-mail from my niece in Florida that said that she and her husband had met a couple that have a home in France and had made the most amazing dinners with many courses plus wines that complimented the meal. "I would love assistance from you on low cost great wine that I can purchase for the next time" she wrote and "can you email me some of your favorite wine." I was very pleased by this request because this is the first time in the fifty plus years that I have known my niece, Carol, that she was showing an interest in the finer aspects of western culture and in this case flattered because she had asked me for help.

I simply wrote off the top of my head the following advice:

> There is no easy way to learn about wine other than drinking it, you just have to drink a large variety!! For someone just getting started I would suggest the following: 1. European wines are invariably a better bargain than US from any state. There are good California wines but not in the less expensive ones. I do like Zinfandel with spicy food and Pinot Noir from Washington state. 2. French wines are becoming expensive so I suggest Spanish red but not white. 3. South American wines are often bitter but I like the Argentine Malbec and Carmenere. 4. We usually don't drink white wine with food but rather chilled Beaujolais from France and Grenache from Spain with seafood. 5. Joyce likes Sauvignon Blanc from South Africa as a before dinner aperitif but sometimes drinks California or New Zealand whites. I suggest that you try the wines mentioned and when you finish doing that you will form opinions of your own. Good luck and if you have questions, just ask.

A few days later I revisited the situation vis-a-vis my advice to Carol and I thought "oh, boy" what a cocky guy I was in my advise. I did not hesitate nor did I give the impression that I might be wrong. Where did these ideas come from and what in my past might qualify me as a wine "expert" in my own mind? Thus I proceeded to review my experience with wine.

I have never taken a wine tasting course nor do I believe in them except as an introduction to the language. Once recently I listened to a wine lecture and realized that the lecturer's knowledge was shallow and in several instances incorrect. Another view of wine courses occurred when I was a professor at Old Dominion University in Norfolk, VA. One of my students took a wine course and for the course's last meeting invited me to attend because they were all going to bring wine and share them. I brought a modest French Chardonnay from the Macon region of Central France. Everyone raved about my wine and when they learned it cost less than ten dollars were stunned. The course had not discussed French or Spanish wines.

I've never been a fan of the smelling, swirling and swishing wine in the mouth to determine its quality. To me, it tastes good, or better, or not good, or awful and price is important. Since I have wine with most meals I find wines for under ten dollars a bottle.

My wine experience began in earnest when my wife and I married 28 years ago. She had in her possession a California Petit Syrah that she had moved from place to place for 15 years. We opened that bottle to compliment a particularly good meal expecting either vinegar or a drinkable wine. We were "blown away" by the quality of this wine. It had aged well. The event unleashed a lifelong interest in wine that began when I was a poor graduate student at the University of Maryland in College Park, MD more than 55 years ago. My busy career did not allow time to appreciate the finer things such as wine. It was work, work, work.

For several years during graduate studies, my first wife and I joined with another couple to enjoy wine and discuss the world. On some Saturdays we would travel to Morris Miller's on Georgia Avenue just within the District of Columbia and purchase six bottles of wine. At that time there were no taxes on wine in D.C. Over a four or five hour period we consumed the wine thus having a good time on Saturday for under ten dollars total. The wines were usually Liebfraumilch, Moselblümchen and Mateus all under $1.50 a bottle.

Bill Bennet, a co-worker at the Applied Physics Lab in Howard County, and his wife Lori were the "another couple". They had met in the navy. She had been a Chief Petty Officer and he an enlisted man of some lower rank. One Saturday night, Lori got drunk and proceeded to march about the room.

Unfortunately two of us were prone on the floor in front of the fireplace and were marched on. The next day I received an apology note for her "unseemly behavior" and a promise that in the future to earnestly endeavor to: "maintain a semblance of sobriety (i.e. no marching), refrain from kicking and abstain from the genial grape", signed penitently (for Lent) Lori Bennet. I still have that note among my prized possessions.

After the Petit Syrah event, I read some books on wine, subscribed to Robert Parker's news letter and consulted my British friend Jake. Robert Parker is a Baltimore lawyer who gave up law in favor of wine. His news letter is named the "Wine Advocate" which is a play on words since the French word for lawyer is avocat. He is now world famous and is considered to have a "palate of gold". Jake was a geologist who had a large and well stocked wine cellar and a keen interest in the geology of wine. When Jake was in D.C. for the 1989 International Geological Conference my wife and I accompanied him to a wine store where under his guidance I selected ten inexpensive wines for our "starter kit". Subsequent to that time we accompanied Jake and his partner Ray on visits to Burgundy, Alsace, Beaujolais and the Loire Valley.

On the tour of Burgundy, I remember that we dropped Jake off at a vineyard one day so that he could measure angles of the sun for a book he was planning on the geology of wine. His partner, Ray, my wife Joyce and I proceeded to the town of Baune to tour the town, sip wine, eat lunch and people watch. Midafternoon we returned to the vineyard, picked up Jake and went to our rooms for a nap before dinner. It was a wine education by drinking and a delightful day.

Since that beginning in 1989, my wife and I have had wine with our food every day unless the food was very spicy. We regularly buy our wine at Calvert Woodley on Connecticut Avenue, five to eight cases at a time. This store has a wide selection of international and domestic wines.

The first of the five points I make in my advice to Carol says that European wines are invariably a better bargain than wines produced in the United States. My reasons are that the wine producing areas of France, Italy and the Iberian Peninsula have produced wine for about 6 thousand years thus the knowledge of wine production is highly evolved and widely known among the population. Culturally wine is routinely served with meals and it is considered a necessity. In Europe competition keeps the wine price low for the everyday wines but these everyday wines must be good in order to be sold.

In the US, wine is more of a recreational activity. Wine is served at social events as an alternative to beer and liquor. People often order wine with their meals when they dine out but don't have wine with their meals at home. Exceptions to this are families with a strong French, Italian or other southern European heritage and a few weird people such as my wife and I.

French wines are the international standard of fine wine. Because of this the prices of French wines have increased over the last several decades as the middle class in China and India can afford more luxury and wish to demonstrate their new status. If one wishes to find good wines for under $10 per bottle, one place to look is among the Spanish wines. Spain has a rich wine history of producing and drinking table wine for daily use and therefore many Spanish wines are excellent and inexpensive.

Wines from Chile and Argentina have a checkered history. Two decades ago they produced some good cabernet sauvignon for the US market. Once they had established a market here the quality seemed to diminish and the wines became mediocre. Two new varietals from Argentina and Chile, Malbec and Carbenere show great promise at this time. Will the history of the Cabernet sauvignon repeat, or will these wines continue to please?

White wines grown in the northern parts of France, the Macon (chardonnay) and the Loire Valley (sauvignon blanc) are excellent but wine from further south seldom please me. White table wines from southern France, Spain, Italy, Argentina and Chile seem tanic and bitter. Other than the Loire Valley and Macon regions of France, white wines are excellent from South Africa and to a lesser extent

New Zealand. We no longer take white wine with seafood but prefer fruitier wines such as gamay or grenache well chilled which serve as an excellent accompaniment to seafood. My wife likes white wines as a before dinner drink and she prefers the Sauvignon Blanc from France, South Africa or California. Another white worthy of mention is from Southwest France and is made from the Picpoul de Pinet grape. Even I like these inexpensive white wines.

My qualifications as a wine guru are minimal and the above history tells all there is to know about my source of knowledge. But then, my goal is to have a good glass of wine with each meal and to influence no one. Take my advice about wine at your own peril.

Pleasures in Bordeaux

O N A VISIT to Bordeaux, France to see the sites and perhaps to buy wine to ship home at a bargain, Joyce and I had a wonderful New Year's Eve dinner and learned more about wine. The one week trip was during my winter break between semesters and included New Year's Eve.

The first priority was to arrange a New Year's Eve meal that included several of our favorite foods. Many restaurants offered exactly the meal we desired but the price was 700-900 French Francs ($126-$172) each. Oh my God! That was much more than we could afford.

Walking away from the center of town, away from the tourist area, away from the more affluent parts until we reached the river where we found, sitting about 400 yards back, the Hotel Basque. Its menu "fit the bill" so we made reservations. Everything we wanted at 400 French Francs ($72) each.

That night we arrived early by French standards, about eight. The first of seven courses was pate d' foix gras followed by oysters on the half shell. Next came half a lobster each then the main course of confit du canard with peas and a salad. The food was accompanied by two full bottles of wine, an Entre deux Mers white, and a good red Bordeaux.

A cheese course followed. We were stuffed by the time dessert was served so when it turned out to be canned fruit cocktail, we just laughed and ate it. Coffee finished one of our most satisfying meals.

The next three days we walked around the city. On New Year's Day everything was closed so we walked through some of the neighborhoods. The following two days were spent visiting museums and searching for wine bargains at the Maison de Vin. Joyce had a lengthy conversation with a young Barton of the famous Barton family that produces several first growth wines. Lunch was wonderful at a small mom and son brasserie on the river. Joyce still talks about the green beans—the best she has ever had.

We visited a privately owned small wine museum called the Musee de Chartronne which featured old wine bottling machines with slides of wine bottling when it was all done by hand. The museum's owner was excited to have visitors during the off season and when he learned that I was a geologist he returned with a tray of gravel. His point was that this gravel was from six feet below the surface and the vines struggled to reach the water there. This stressed the vines and made them stronger so that they produced superior wine making grapes.

We returned to Paris by train the next day. No wine to ship home because a $400 license was required. No wine, but wonderful memories of a fantastic New Year's Eve feast. All in all, the trip was a good deal.

Amuse Bouche

URING THE 1990s my wife, Joyce, and I visited the French port city of Nantes at the mouth of the Loire River. Each time we went we spent one day at La Baule, a beach on the Atlantic that required a one hour train ride. The train station was six or eight blocks inland from the shoreline. The beach itself was sandy and about two hundred yards wide and separated from the businesses by a road. This road had heavy traffic during the summer months but perhaps not so much off season.

One particular day we exited the train station to walk the six or eight blocks to the beach. On our way, we saw a basset hound come out of a side street headed for the beach. As he got closer to the road we worried that he would be hit by one of the fast moving cars. The dog just walked up to the road unconcerned and crossed the road. He was not hit and the traffic was not inconvenienced. It was like a miracle!

My Fifteen Minutes
of Fame

THE TERM "FIFTEEN minutes of fame" was first used in 1968 by Andy Warhol when he said "In the future everyone will be world-famous for 15 minutes."

Some ways in which a person can have 15 minutes of fame are classic. If you win the mega-lottery for more than $100,000 the world will know about it and then quickly forget. Killing a parent, sibling or child will be known to all for about fifteen minutes.

Classic fame results when an individual works in his or her field for any years and wins a Nobel Prize. A baseball player who hits more than 100 home runs during his career is famous to many baseball players.

I believe my "fifteen minutes of fame" lasted about 15 minutes. The following describes what happened.

I was sitting in my office preparing my next lecture for some graduate course I was teaching that semester. I was a professor of Geology at Old Dominion University in Norfolk, VA. I received a phone call and the person wanted to ask about my research on sampling in the fossil record. His name was Robert Lewin, an editorial writer for *Science* magazine. I did not recognize the name. Being proud of my research I answered the questions and when he was finished I returned to my lecture preparation.

Several weeks later I received a phone call from a young lady asking for a recent black and white photo. She identified herself as the secretary for Roger Lewin who wrote editorials for *Science*, the premier publication of scientific research in the United States. I did not have a black and white photo less than 15 years old so I sent her that one.

On 1 May, 1987 a rather complementary piece by Roger Lewin appeared in *Science*. Two weeks later I received a letter from a colleague at Franklin and Marshall College named R.D.K. Thomas. He said that he appreciated my paper and that he found it "most helpful."

In August, 1987 I was interviewed by a writer for *Image,* the magazine of Northern California which is included in the *San Francisco Examiner* on Sundays. He wrote an article titled: "Bone Wars" about the controversy between Richard Leakey and Donald Johanson with regards to the famous fossil human named Lucy. I am quoted in the article as saying that "Paleo-anthropologists often make too much of a little bit of information" and "when they find a new fossil, well, that changes ideas of what they saw in the past" and "that's only because they draw too detailed a picture in the first place."

I would not have known about this article had not a colleague read it on a plane, saved it and sent it to me. This raises the possibility that other articles have been written utilizing my research.

In any event, my "fifteen minutes of fame" began with the *Science* editorial of 1 May, 1987 and ended sometime in the late summer 1987.

Shopping for A
Paris Picnic

A FAVORITE PARIS meal of my wife Joyce and I is a picnic on the banks of the Seine. It features a rotisserie chicken accompanied by wine, bread, cheese and fruit. A warm sunny day is helpful.

The French are very careful about food quality and each picnic component is purchased at a shop staffed by someone knowledgeable of the food type. I know of no supermarkets or comprehensive grocery stores in Paris.

Our hotel room in the left bank Latin Quarter is within three blocks of the nearest Metro station and seven blocks from the Seine. All of the shops required are within one hundred yards of the Metro and on the way to the river bank.

The rotisserie chicken is bought at an *epicerie*, a food store offering miscellaneous items. The rotisserie consists of chickens in rows of 8 rotating in front of an electric heater such that they baste the chickens in the rows below. The vendor will remove one of the juicy golden brown, well cooked chickens from the rotisserie and hand it to the customer in a wax paper bag.

Next stop is the cheese shop or *fromagerie*. This open front store, smelling just as you would expect from the assortment of stinky cheeses offered, displays many cheese varieties in their on-street displays and has an additional one hundred or so cheeses inside. A white aproned cheese expert will guide your purchase if asked and can tell you when a soft cheese like brie or Camembert will be ready. A hard cheese is more manageable at the picnic site, so we usually select a block of ivory colored French Emmethal cheese. Charles de Gaulle once lamented on managing a country that produces over 400 cheeses.

Next to the *fromagerie*, is Cuvier's wine business. The name Cuvier is especially dear to me since George Cuvier was one of paleontology's pioneers and I am a paleontologist. Many varieties of less expensive wines are displayed in the front of the shop and the most expensive kept in the back. We always select a red wine that we know well, usually a Cote du Rhone.

We bypass the next two shops which sell meat and seafood. The fruit and vegetable store is next. A rainbow of colorful items all displayed in perfect rows awaits us. Even the very small strawberries are in a row. We select a large fragrant orange newly arrived from Spain.

Then we cross the street to the *boulangerie*, bread store, to buy a fresh from the oven baguette. Inside this store they display various types of bread and rolls. I prefer the slimmest baguette for our picnic, more crust per pound.

We now have everything we need for the picnic since we always travel with a corkscrew, wooden handled French picnic knife, called an Opinal and a bath towel from our hotel room to spread out. We travel a few blocks to the river bank, select a suitable site to eat and watch the boats go by in the shadow of Notre Dame. It doesn't get better than this.

Los Angeles, 1957

O N SUNDAY MAY 5, 1957, the day after I received my B.S. in Electrical Engineering at the University of Maryland's graduation ceremony, I took my first business trip. I had been working for a small company in Beltsville, MD named Davies Laboratory for about six months. After the first three months the company was purchased by Minneapolis Honeywell. A short time later Honeywell also purchased the rights to manufacture a digital data acquisition system developed by Rocketdyne at their rocket test facility in the San Gabriel Mountains north of Los Angeles, California.

Accompanied by an experienced engineer named Bill Popowski the two of us left from Friendship

Airport, now BWI, on the first jet plane that I had ever experienced. To me, the plane seemed to gain altitude almost vertically and I could feel myself pressed back in my seat. We took a room in the "valley" just south of the San Gabriel Mountains and the following day visited the Rocketdyne test facility. We were hosted by Dr. Martin Klein, developer of the digital data acquisition system and also the "science guy" on a local LA TV station. He was a very personable gentleman and I remember that in the conversations we had about things other than the system, he told me "never trust a Hungarian". Of course, he was of Hungarian descent. This was the beginning of an idea I developed that subject people by necessity learned to be clever and in some cases devious in order to survive.

This was the first digital data acquisition system in the world. Prior to that time, the instruments were analog and the data could not easily be converted to a form that could take advantage of the increasingly powerful digital computers. Dr. Klein's system utilized an analog to digital converter shared by many sensors which were multiplexed. He named it "the Idiot" system. This was Dr. Klein's way of asserting to the public that computers were not smart and could only perform tasks exactly as told.

After learning about the system's workings for several days, we left the San Gabriel Mountains and drove to the Rocketdyne manufacturing facility in Long Beach to copy the plans and drawings. We were confronted with the formidable task of copying several thousands of pages. Being inherently lazy I talked them into letting us borrow the plans for a short time so that they could be copied by our people in Maryland. This freed up most of a day and we chose to spend the found time visiting Disneyland in nearby Anaheim. Disneyland was only half completed at the time. There was no Matterhorn but I recall there was the Adventureland cruise, Aunt Jemima's Pancake House, and the Maxwell House Coffee Shop. I can only imagine what wonderful features have been added to Disneyland in the last 58 years.

There were many superb restaurants in the valley and my previous experiences eating out were limited to Bar-B-Q, Hot Shoppes and the Langlin, a Chinese restaurant in Langley Park. Bill Popowski liked good restaurants and by accompanying him I managed to spend most of my per diem in the first three days. My solution was an all-you-can-eat restaurant that featured prime rib. Because I was recently a college student, this arrangement was perfect for me. However, I gained over ten pounds in one week.

This trip was educational, rewarding and enjoyable. I marvel now that I have never been back to Los Angeles in the intervening sixty-five years.

A Huge "Little Favor"

AHMED HOSSINI WAS a student in my Historical Geology class in the spring of 1979. That January, the citizens of Iran revolted against the rule of the U.S. Backed Shah Pahlavi and there was great turmoil in that country. When time came for the final exam Ahmed, an Iranian, came to my office and asked if I would give him the grade of Incomplete so that he could return to Iran and bring his mother to the U.S. To live with him and his brother. The time for which you could drop a course without getting a failing grade had passed a month earlier but I agreed to his request.

In July he came to my office and asked if he could take the final then because he was a senior in Business Administration and needed a science course to graduate in the fall. I suggested that he review his notes and return in one week to take the exam. He returned, took the exam and when I graded the exam he had not quite achieved a passing grade.

I'm not sure why I let that fact slide and gave him a passing grade. Ideas that passed through my mind were that he was not a geology major and therefore would not embarrass our program, that he was a senior and my grade allowed him to graduate, and he had recently had the stress of rescuing his mother. I didn't say "you failed but I let it slide" I simply told him "you passed." He thanked me profusely for allowing him to take the test late and invited me to the restaurant at the Kingsmill Country Club in Williamsburg, a mere twenty miles from Norfolk, where he was the "Maitre d". I soon forgot the whole affair.

The situation in Iran worsened in 1979. Fifty-two Americans were taken hostage at the U.S. Embassy in Tehran. They were held until January 20, 1981. This "hostage situation" led to the defeat of Jimmy Carter and the election of Ronald Reagan in 1980.

About four years after I allowed Ahmed to take a make up exam, my younger brother Charles, accepted a position as a law professor at The College of William and Mary. When a young lady that he had been dating at his previous position in Chicago came to visit he invited my wife and me to join then at Kingsmill Restaurant. We accepted.

After a premeal cocktail we ordered our meal. While waiting for the ladies to make up their minds I told our waiter that I had had a student named Ahmed Hossini who worked at this restaurant several years ago and inquired if he was still around.

The waiter said that Ahmed still worked there running the kitchen. "Give him regards from Professor Koch if you see him," I said. The appetizers arrived at our table followed by several appetizers we had not ordered. The meal arrived accompanied by several luscious side dishes that were not listed on the menu. After the meal, with our coffee came a complimentary dessert made from apples and nuts and lit aflame at the table. This dish was accompanied by a very nice Sauterne perfectly matching the dessert's sweetness. After cocktails, two bottles of wine with dinner, a dessert wine and complimentary Cognac we didn't argue about anything. We simply asked for the check.

Surprisingly the check had been paid. Charles and I estimated the approximate amount and tipped the waiter accordingly. My guess was that it was important to Ahmed that he repay me for my small act of kindness. I thought that a bottle of wine would have been more in line with the situation. I did not see Ahmed that night nor ever again.

The reader may ask "where is the epiphany?" The epiphany came years later when I realized what was to me a small act of kindness was huge to the recipient of that kindness. So I keep that in mind.

East Berlin, 1987

I STUDIED FOSSILS at the Humboldt Museum in East Berlin about two years before the famous "Berlin Wall" came down. It was one of the museums that I visited that year as part of a National Geographic Society grant to study the European uppermost Cretaceous bivalve species to determine the number of species that were in common with the United States. The trip began in the spring and lasted four months. During that time I visited seven other museums and took five field trips to various localities from which some of the fossils had been collected.

I arrived in Templehof Airport mid-day and shared a cab with a West German businessman to the famous checkpoint Charlie, the point of entry to

East Berlin. This West German was staying in East Berlin because it was the 750th anniversary of Berlin's founding and all hotels in the west were booked. At checkpoint Charlie I converted West German marks for East German marks at parity even though the real value of the East German mark was about one tenth. But they had you.

The very large and heavy luggage I had contained thousands of photos of U.S. fossil bivalves and a few clothes. Halfway to my hotel the luggage wheels gave out and I began to carry it. After a few blocks a German couple with a child gave me a ride. They were quite friendly and seemed to enjoy the opportunity to be helpful to an American.

The Palast Hotel on the east end of Unter Den Linden, the showcase boulevard of Berlin, was a modern hotel built about one year earlier to attract westerners. They took my passport and kept it for three days. Every building looked great along Unter Den Linden however, just one block over several of the buildings remained bombed out. They had not been repaired in the intervening 42 years.

At the Humboldt the workers were afraid to be seen as friendly to an American. Each morning I took an elevator to the fourth floor where I stayed without company or the ability to leave without calling for the door to be unlocked. I studied the fossil collections making notes about similarities between those from Europe and the pictures I carried. At lunch time I was "let out" to eat. I usually ate alone but on one occasion and one occasion only a nice young English speaking German woman shared her table with me and we had an interesting conversation about the U.S.

One day when I finished early, I walked to the nearby Kochstrasse to view the birthplace of Robert Koch, a famous German scientist of the late 19th century and possible relative. Credited as one of the founders of bacteriology and microbiology, he investigated the anthrax disease cycles and studied the bacteria that causes tuberculosis and cholera. There was a statue of him on the square and when I took a picture all hell broke loose. Cars came down the street from both directions, several policemen jumped out and yelled at me in German. When I answered in English, they asked me for my passport. When I told them I was an American professor named Koch visiting the Humboldt they threw up their hands. Ahh, professors are not practical and have no understanding of reality, they quipped. They returned my passport and wished me a good day. I was fortunate that the hotel had returned my passport the day before. In taking the picture, my camera was pointed directly at the Berlin Wall from their side.

I was able to repair my suitcase using a garden hose clamp, and checked out of the Palast. At checkpoint Charlie I inquired about exchanging my marks. Each step through the process I was told that their exchange was further on. At the end—no money exchange. The visit to East Berlin left me with two things, the impression that the government was behaving better vis-a-vis their people and the west, and a pocket full of expensive but worthless East German marks.

Time Travel: Back 20 M.Y.A (Twenty Million Years Ago)

T WAS A cold, cloudy March morning on the Chesapeake Bay in 1969 and the sun had just come up. I was walking along the Calvert Cliffs just south of Chesapeake Beach when I noticed a dark brown bone fragment in the cliff wall about shoulder high. Digging around where the bone was exposed led me to the discovery of many porpoise teeth and bones. Why was I there at that place at that time?

My career to date as an electrical engineer was rewarding and successful but I wanted a career that allowed me to travel and be outdoors more often.

I started taking Geology courses at The George Washington University to pursue a PhD with a specialty in Paleontology. It seemed prudent to gain practical experience for the activities that the new career might require. I bought a Bronco to gain experience operating an off road vehicle and I visited localities within 75 miles that had interesting rocks or fossils.

The Calvert Cliffs were a frequent destination and I soon learned that the winter months yielded more fossils. This was because very few other people were looking for fossils at that time and the cliffs were sloughing off sediment containing fossils at a higher rate. I had been a duck hunter most of my life and therefore I had the warm clothes and hip boots to survive the winter weather.

As I dug around the dark bone fragments I encountered more bones and some porpoise teeth. Digging carefully about one foot into the cliffs, I carved out two blocks of sediment about ten inches by fourteen inches and encased these blocks in plaster of paris. I had accompanied Al Myrich, the porpoise collector for the Smithsonian, several times and knew how to prepare a sample. I took these two blocks home to dry so I could check for teeth and bones at a later time

The sediment was a blue-gray clay with some fine grained sand. When I dug into the cliffs the clay smelled unlike any other clay I have smelled before because it had been deposited on the sea bottom.

There were apparently more bones in the hole but after six hours of digging I ran out of time and I was tired. I made the hole look as though nothing remained by trashing the edges and went home.

The next Saturday morning I returned to the hole. Digging further back I discovered the porpoise's jaws and some of the cranium in a vertical position. It was as though the porpoise was thrown during a strong storm "like a fat dart" into the sea bottom. Further, all of the other bones and teeth seemed to be in a single layer. I encased the jaws in plaster and removed them. In addition I removed two more blocks of sediment encased in plaster. Again I made the hole appear empty.

I began to worry that someone might find the hole and check for more bones. I knew that there were more bones. Three days later I returned to the hole with help. Tom Wright of the National Science Foundation and his wife Suse provided the help I needed. Tom and I excavated and encased in plaster 6 more blocks of sediment and these blocks later yielded the top of the cranium that had been encrusted with barnacles and many more bones and teeth.

Suse occupied herself while we worked by reading the paper and walking the beach. She found one of the largest (about 4 inches) light colored, perfect sharks tooth I have ever seen—not fair! Tom and I also left the hole appearing to be empty.

I returned alone the next Saturday, removed four more encased sediment blocks from the back of the hole. More ribs and vertebrae were found. I checked the hole to make certain no more material could be found. The hole had grown to be over 5 feet deep by 7 feet wide. A virtual cave.

In the process of checking for more material I crawled completely into the cave. When I looked out it was as though I was at the time when the sediments were deposited, that is twenty million years back. The unusual smell of the clay, the dampness, the limited view of the present gave me the strong feeling of being in the past – very eerie.

After preparing the fifteen plaster encased blocks of sediment at a later time, it became apparent that most of the important bones of one porpoise had been found. That these bones are from a single porpoise is important to the study of porpoise evolution. Missing are the vertebrae from the tail and bones of the vestigial hind limbs. Porpoise hind limbs are lost because these types of animals left land millions of years ago. Found were about 100 teeth, both jaws, cranium, five of six forelimb bones, three of four ear bones (2 outer, 1 inner), most ribs, 18 vertebrae, many smaller bones such as the hyoid and the remains of marine turtles. All of this material was donated to the Smithsonian Museum of Natural History.

Collecting a skull at Wakefield, VA in 1968.
Note the skull is encased in plaster.

Me in my engineering office about 1972. Note the
porpoise jaws displayed on the book shelf to my right.

Beauty in A
Strange Place

CRUNCH, CRACKLE, SQUISH, snap and pop – these are the ugly sounds that welcomed me to Jamaica as I traveled on a dark coastal highway between Montego Bay Airport and the Discovery Bay Marine Lab. Masses of land crabs were migrating across the road in search of a mate and each crackle or snap signaled that a crab had given its all in the search for love. We checked into our rooms that night after a quick snack.

At daylight I could see that I was at the Johns Hopkins Marine Lab on the north coast of Jamaica where college students came to study a coral reef offshore. There were no student groups present so we had the place to ourselves. The other half of the "we" was Tony Coates, a George Washington University professor, my dissertation adviser and friend. He had arranged for me to study the Guinea Corn Formation in central Jamaica as my dissertation subject.

I had finished my course work and comprehensive exams. This field work was the remaining hurdle for a PhD in Geology and was my first effort as a geologist. This represented a major lifestyle change from my twenty year career as an electrical engineer. Further, this was my first trip outside of the U.S. Travel has always been a personal goal and the desire to travel even helped me to decide a career change.

As I left Washington, I was delighted that the House Judiciary Committee had nailed the crooked Richard Nixon. It was only a matter of time before he would leave the White House. How I loathed him for betraying his country for personal power, causing the unnecessary deaths of over 25,000 U.S. military personnel in Viet Nam and as we have subsequently learned – he KNEW the war could not be won. He divided this country between those that served and those that knew the war was wrong.

The next morning Tony left me at the lab while he went to pick up a third scientist – Jim Kennedy, Oxford professor and British Museum adjunct who wished to make bulk collections of fossils for the museum. Jim Kennedy had been an Olympic swimmer for the U.K., Tony Coates was a skilled Rugby player and former cricket professional.

Both men were about five years younger than I and both had over twenty years of experience as a paleontologist/geologist.

While Tony was gone I wandered the grounds, tried my hands rowing and gathered my thoughts vis-a-vis our project. About 4 in the afternoon I witnessed the man that had been doing yard work sit under a palm tree with a rolled newspaper filled with ganja (marijuana) and light up. There must have been more that one pound of weed in that "ciggie". Ganja grows wild in Jamaica.

Next day the three of us got an early start to take advantage of the cooler morning. We went to a small town ten miles south named Shaw Castle where the playground of the elementary school is known to yield fossils by erosion. When we stepped out of the car we heard singing. About 30 or 40 little Jamaican children singing their national anthem in that cool misty morning. It was "the most beautiful sound I've ever heard" lyrics courtesy of West Side Story.

Fortunately the playground had been graded recently and the fossils washed out by rain. We were able to collect two large bags for the British Museum in just two hours.

We then drove about 25 miles to the Guinea Corn Formation along the crystal clear and narrow Rio Minho. The formation's sediments were originally deposited as a one mile thick horizontal pile. Tectonism had moved them to a vertical position. Subsequently these 80 million year old rocks were incised by the Rio Minho such that one could study them at the present time without climbing. There would be no problem for me to measure thickness and collect fossils in the days to come.

The plan was that I would stay with a Peace Corps couple from Ohio that was teaching in a small hilltop community nearby called Spalding, we needed to find Spalding. We inquired of some young men walking along the road if we were on the road to Spalding. The answer was startling – "gawblimy – I dunno – I from Brixton". So the first Jamaican we talked to in the very remotest part of the country was a criminal from south London hiding from the police. I've often wondered what his crime had been – murder?

On to Green Island, on the north coast for a stay at Katy's Bed and Breakfast. We arrived just before dark and she had made oxtail for dinner. I had never had oxtail before but loved its strong beefy flavor. Off to bed after a long hard day of field work.

I was awakened by the sound of a donkey braying, hee haw, hee haw.

Looking out the window at the nearby large beehive shaped hills covered with the greenest vegetation and the donkey's noise in the morning mist was a truly beautiful scenario.

We traveled to a nearby area named Jerusalem Mountain where Tony Coates had been asked by the U.S. Geological Survey to make a map. Before Tony became a George Washington University professor he spent several years teaching at the University of the West Indies near Kingston. He was a sought after expert on much of the Jamaican geology.

That evening, I was dropped off in Spalding. Tony and Jim left for parts unknown, The next morning I went to the outcrops along the Rio Minho and began measuring bed thickness and collecting fossils which I bagged and labeled. I had worked alone for several days when two Land Rovers and five men showed up. The boss was a Dutch national named Jens, working for the Jamaican Geological Survey. Accompanying him were two trainees and two drivers. He hoped to talk to Tony Coates about some Jamaican geology he was studying.

Since he was there and just waiting, his crew commenced to measure the whole section. What a God send for me because this was a tedious task for an individual. He returned a second day looking for Tony but when Tony failed to appear by day's end he left me the measurements and a Land Rover with driver. The driver helped me move the rocks and fossil samples from the river bed to the road in the coming days.

However, during that second day a large and beautiful specimen of a rudist clam was discovered. Jens wanted to display this fossil at the survey's headquarters. We dug around this approximately eighty pound specimen to dislodge it without harm. About half way through the task a local Jamaican joined in the effort.

He was about seventy years old and weighed maybe one hundred and thirty pounds. With shorts and no shoes he presented a wiry and scruffy figure. He jumped into the hole with childlike enthusiasm digging with his hands until the fossil was free—but there was a problem. While he was in the hole two teenage boys stole his bag of mangoes. He screamed at them. They threatened him and got in his face. He maneuvered the confrontation around until he could reach his ten foot walking stick. Then with 'wildlife speed" he wacked one of the boys on the shoulder so hard that it may have been broken. He had childlike enthusiasm but he was a "man". This was beautiful to witness.

The weeks went by and I finished my data collecting. The bags of fossils, measured section, notes, field boots and tools were packed in a shipping trunk to be sent to Washington, DC. This was the end of the research project until I and the shipping trunk returned to Washington.

Tony and I flew to San Juan, Puerto Rico and had dinner with another colleague, Norm Sohl, with the U. S. Geological Survey. Ironically, I had land crab for dinner, considering how the land crabs had welcomed me to Jamaica. The three of us flew to the French island of Guadeloupe to attend a Caribbean geologic conference. We stayed at the posh Meridian Hotel and dined on fine French cuisine. Talk about a contrast with my four weeks on the Rio Minho. In

Guadeloupe I learned to love the beauty of a French beach and the taste of Guava paste.

Soon after I returned to Washington, Richard Nixon resigned as president and returned to California in disgrace. I was overjoyed.

The shipping trunk and all the work that its contents represented was never seen again. Perhaps some Jamaican saw it on the dock and thought it contained valuables. We will never know. I self-funded a research field trip to Western Kansas and Colorado, wrote a dissertation, graduated and took a job at the Old Dominion University in Norfolk, VA teaching geology and paleontology. Over the next 22 years I published innumerable papers in scientific journals and gave research results at about 70 professional meetings. By the time I retired, I had a strong international reputation for good research and the academic rank of full professor. I traveled widely. The Jamaican trip marked the very beginning of this rewarding second career.

Why Paleo?

ARLY IN 1978, I moved from the Washington DC area to Norfolk, Virginia to begin a career as an Old Dominion University professor of geology. Prior to that I had worked as an electrical engineer for various companies over a twenty year period. The last position was as the manager of a small computer organization that served the Seismic Data Lab funded by ARPA. The career as a geology professor fulfilled my desires to teach, to travel and to work outdoors from time to time. None of these three activities were available regularly when I worked as an electrical engineer.

Teaching has given me great satisfaction in the past. When I volunteered for the Marine Corp during the Korean War, I was tested by the Marine

Corp and found to have a fairly high I.Q. They sent me to the Navy's aviation electronics school NATTC in Millington, TN for a seven month course. When I finished the course, they then assigned me to be an electronics instructor. For the last 28 months of my enlistment I taught and I took great satisfaction in knowing that the students learned a great deal. I loved teaching and vowed to teach again someday.

Travel had been on my "bucket list" since the age of eight. That is when I began avidly collecting postage stamps. Stamps from times gone by and stamps from foreign countries fascinated me.

One winter when I was about twelve, it snowed heavily. The area in which I lived was hilly and many of the roads serving the steeper streets were impassable. This was a problem for the Holmes Bakery truck driver because many of his regular customers could not be reached by truck that day and they depended on him for their bread. The bakery truck driver paid me five dollars to walk to these homes. After a long, hard day trudging through the snow, I went home and bought some foreign stamps that had been sent to me "on approval" and added them to my collection. I vividly remember one of the most popular songs at that time was "Managua, Nicaragua". Whenever I hear that song I remember the snowy day that I jumped bread.

You can imagine my disappointment when I joined the Marine Corp with visions of Japan and Korea only to have the visions vanish when I was sent to Millington, TN for almost three years.

My love of the outdoors and wild animals had always been part of my soul. It grew immensely during the ages of fourteen and eighteen because every weekend of those four years were spent with my father either hunting, fishing or trapping fur bearing animals for profit. We hunted squirrel in Greenbelt and Glendale, ducks along the Potomac at Port Tobacco, rabbits and quail near Welcome, MD and several times geese on the eastern shore. When there was no hunting season we fished in Tridelphia and Rocky Gorge reservoirs, South River and the Chesapeake Bay. Trapping season lasted from January 1 to March 15th and we tended our traps before dawn every day. We caught several hundred muskrats and about fifty mink, skinned them, stretched and dried the fur, and sent the pelts to Sears Roebuck raw fur market for money.

My interest in animals, birds and fish grew along with my love of the woods and streams. If one is to be a successful hunter, trapper or fisherman, he must know the life habit of his prey. It's easy to understand my concentration on paleontology within the geology discipline. In paleontology we study not only the animal per se, but its ecological patterns, evolutionary history and distribution.

My career as a college professor fulfilled all of my needs. I taught 8 different courses from the introductory to upper graduate level, presented over 2000 lectures. I traveled to all parts of the US and eleven foreign countries to present papers about my research. My research required field trips to Southwest US and Northwest Europe. My students and I made field trips to outcrops of various geological ages in Virginia, Maryland and North Carolina. During these travels I made a few close personal friendships in the US and Europe that continue to this day.

During those twenty years, 70 of my articles were published. One 1991 paper in the international journal, <u>Historical Geology</u> received a very rare review because it was described by the reviewers as "flawless." Another paper in <u>Paleobiology</u> was notable enough to warrant a feature article in <u>Science,</u> May, 1987 because of its impact on evolutionary ideas. Another moment of pride came when a colleague named a Pliocene snail <u>Echphora kochi.</u>

My career as a geology professor was successful on many counts, but none of that explains "Why Paleo?" After all I could have had an equally satisfying career in some other science, particularly Zoology. Here is the truth. I have had this beard since 1962 and did not want to shave it off. Fossils never have an odor because the smelly parts disappear with age, there was not a chance of my beard taking on an unpleasant aroma. I always imagined that a bearded zoologist went home every night with the smell of formaldehyde on his beard. This idea was the final consideration for the decision to make paleontology my life's work.

My Unusual Retirement

S A FACULTY member, paleontologist and professionally active individual, my complete retirement from these activities is unusual. Normally an academician will remain near his institution and participate as emeritus faculty in the life of the university. Most scientists continue their research, writing results of previous investigations and initiating studies on his personal bucket list. An individual involved in the affairs of the relevant society will retain his membership and attends annual meetings. I did none of these because I was burned out by life to date.

A Toe's Tale

"IT WAS A dark and stormy night; the rain fell in torrents—except.." (Bulwer-Lytten and Clifford, 1830) and that night I was lying in the middle of Columbia Road about 100 yards west of 18th ST. NW, Washington, DC having been both knocked down and run over by an SUV. The driver, a woman in her mid-thirties remained on the scene and was mortified. Before we leave this scene to chronicle the three previous hours I must confess that it was raining only lightly. The use of the famous opening line is justified by the fact that both Snoopy and I love the way it sounds.

The story of how I happened to be lying in the road begins three hours earlier. My wife, Joyce and I drove from our home in Annapolis to the Mintwood

Place restaurant on Columbia Road made famous by several positive reviews from Tom Sietsema of the Washington Post. We parked on the street opposite the restaurant, entered the place and selected a quiet booth for dinner. In a few minutes we were joined by one of Joyce's former co-workers in Labor and Delivery at DePaul Hospital, Norfolk, VA. Kathy Bentley and her daughter Caitlin, whose apartment was five or six blocks east of the restaurant. When she suggested Mintwood as a meeting place and dinner we jumped at the opportunity. Joyce and Kathy had not seen each other for over 16 years.

We all had an aperitif, appetizers, entree and dessert. The wine and the conversation flowed effortlessly between the ladies mostly about where former co-workers are located at present. After a two and a half hour meal we exited the restaurant back into the "dark and lightly raining night".

The three ladies preceded me across the street to the car chatting and gesturing, traffic was very light and I was delayed waiting for a car from the left to pass. When I was nearly across the street, a black SUV that was double parked, suddenly backed up just as I was passing behind it. It ran over the toes of my left foot and the side mirror knocked me down. I screamed "she backed up" on the way down and she stopped. Somehow tire tracks decorated my trousers.

Joyce and Kathy Bentley came back to help me but since I was NOT having a baby, the L&D nurse and the midwife were barely more help than a layman! Three young people identified themselves as last year medical students and offered to help. The driver suggested that she call 911. My answer was "please help me up and I'll see if there is any damage".

Upon standing, I declared "no harm, no foul" and that nothing seemed to be broken. Joyce wanted me to go to the Emergency Room to be checked out I assured her that everything was fine and that several hours in an emergency room to double check was not worth the trouble. We bid all good night and returned to Annapolis.

The harm proved to be minimal. My big toe and the two adjacent turned deep black but after several months the discoloration disappeared.

My left toe has had an interesting eighty four years having been run over once before as well as having a hammer dropped on it. If the toe were to write its tale, it certainly would have to start "it was a dark and stormy night".

About the Author

The author grew up in the Maryland suburbs of Washington, D.C. He has lived in Maryland all his life except for three years as a Electronics Instructor in the Marine Corps while stationed in Millington, TN. Upon leaving Millington he earned a Masters Degree in Electrical Engineering at the University of Maryland. In 1972 he obtained a PhD in Geology and spent 20 years as a full professor at Old Dominion University in Norfolk, VA teaching Historical Geology and Paleontology courses. While a professor he wrote a number of refereed papers in Scientific Journals and at Collington he wrote a number of personal memoirs as part of a memoir writing class.

Upon retirement he moved to Annapolis, MD where he lived for 12 years and then moved to Collington, a Retirement Community in Mitchellville, MD where he now resides with his wife Joyce.